MANAGERS
FOR
THE YEAR 2000

MANAGERS

FOR

THE YEAR 2000

WILLIAM H. NEWMAN, Editor

SAMUEL BRONFMAN PROFESSOR
OF DEMOCRATIC BUSINESS ENTERPRISE
GRADUATE SCHOOL OF BUSINESS
COLUMBIA UNIVERSITY

57564

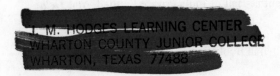
PRENTICE-HALL, INC., ENGLEWOOD CLIFFS, NEW JERSEY 07632

Library of Congress Cataloging in Publication Data
Main entry under title:

Managers for the year 2000.

    Based on papers presented at a symposium held on the
occasion of the 25th anniversary of the establishment
of the Samuel Bronfman Chair in Democratic Business
Enterprise at Columbia University Graduate School of
Business, in April 1976.

    Bibliography: p.
    1. Industrial management—Congresses. 2. Economic
forecasting—Congresses. I. Newman, William Herman,
(date). II. Samuel Bronfman Foundation, New York.
HD29.M33   658.4   77-15458
ISBN 0-13-549378-1

Printed in the United States of America

10 9 8 7 6 5 4 3 2

Prentice-Hall International, Inc., *London*
Prentice-Hall of Australia Pty. Limited, *Sydney*
Prentice-Hall of Canada, Ltd., *Toronto*
Prentice-Hall of India Private Limited, *New Delhi*
Prentice-Hall of Japan, Inc., *Tokyo*
Prentice-Hall of Southeast Asia Pte. Ltd., *Singapore*
Whitehall Books Limited, *Wellington, New Zealand*

CONTENTS

CONTRIBUTORS

Theodore J. Gordon is President of The Futures Group, a consulting organization that makes technological, social, and economic forecasts for business and government. Gordon is one of the world's most sophisticated and scientifically based futurologists.

Marvin Bower, a director of McKinsey & Company, served as the firm's Managing Director during the period when it developed its worldwide reputation for consultation to senior management. Bower personally has counseled top managers in many leading U.S. corporations.

Eli Ginzberg is an international authority on manpower. In his role as Director of the Conservation of Human Resources Project at Columbia University, he has authored or co-authored more than twenty books on various aspects of manpower. Among his many public roles, he is currently serving as Chairman of the National Commission for Manpower Policy.

Anthony C. Hubert is Secretary General of the European Association of National Productivity Centres. He also serves as Editor of the journal, *International Management Development.* In these roles he has become familiar with management development activities throughout Europe.

Robert K. Greenleaf had a long and distinguished career in A.T.&T. He was primarily responsible for many of the Bell System's pioneering efforts in executive development and is regarded as one of the most profound thinkers about the managing of business enterprises.

Harold F. Smiddy was the major architect of the reorganization of General Electric Company under Ralph Cordiner's regime. As a part of that movement, he launched the Company's Crotonville campus for executive training and sponsored what is undoubtedly one of the outstanding executive education efforts in history. He has been active in a variety of management societies, serving as President of the Academy of Management, and is a recipient of the Taylor Key.

W. Allen Wallis is currently Chancellor of the University of Rochester. He served for six years as Dean of the Graduate School of Business, University of Chicago, and was a prime mover in building that School as a strong center for quantitative approaches to business problems.

Samuel Bronfman Fellows. Each year since autumn of 1951 Columbia University has awarded five Bronfman Fellowships to outstanding students in its Graduate School of Business. These are among the most prestigious awards in the School. Now over one hundred former Bronfman Fellows are employed in widely diversified jobs throughout the world. This group served as a panel to critique the papers presented at the symposium.

William H. Newman (Editor) is Samuel Bronfman Professor of Democratic Business Enterprise at Columbia's Graduate School of Business. He pioneered Columbia's Arden House executive programs, and has been active in many other company and university management development activities—both in the United States and abroad. His books on management are widely used and have been translated into eight foreign languages.

iNTROduCTiON

Aim ANd StRUCTURE of STUdy

World events are moving at a giddy pace. Peasants in remote villages now see on television the splendor and the slums of New York and Tokyo. Weak nations become powerful almost overnight; empires crumble. Technology gives us new industries and shatters others. Even more basic is the change in values and ethics. Increasingly, we turn to government intervention, yet we are doubtful that our democratic institutions will respond wisely. It may be trite to say we live in a world of rapid change, but is very true—and important.

Enterprises—corporations, small firms, not-for-profit ventures —are our main instruments for relating the actual creation of goods and services to this bubbling environment. They are the intermediaries between the work each of us performs and the markets where resources are assembled and output distributed. They are the centers of initiative and of action. Unless these enterprises are well managed, unless they adjust wisely to the shifting environment, our complex, pluralistic system will collapse.

The question addressed in this short book is: What should be done now to prepare enterprise managers for the world ahead? Are we, in our colleges and companies, developing future managers with the qualifications that will be crucial during the period when they hold the reins?

"Managers for the year 2000" sounds remote. To many people

the turn of the century seems too far away to prepare for. Yet simple arithmetic shows that the men and women presently in colleges and universities will be in the prime of their careers in 2000. So in the management education arena the time to think about the needs of the next century has already arrived. Companies focus on a shorter planning horizon. Nevertheless, most of the forces we shall examine will not wait on the calendar; they are already emerging. For companies, also, "It is later than you think."

To provide perspective the present report is divided into four parts:

I. Shape of the world . . . in the year 2000
II. Characteristics of managers . . . needed in the year 2000
III. Sources of management talent . . . for the year 2000
IV. Who should do what . . . to prepare for the year 2000?

A symposium was held at Columbia University following this same format. Distinguished authorities submitted papers on each of the topics; these papers were discussed, and later additional proposals were made. This report presents the papers and the penetrating reactions they evoked.

The specific occasion for the symposium was the 25th anniversary of the establishment of the Samuel Bronfman Chair in Democratic Business Enterprise at Columbia University's Graduate School of Business. Each year since the Chair was created, five outstanding students have held Samuel Bronfman Fellowships. These men and women now hold key positions in widely diverse organizations, and we used them as the panel for the symposium discussions. Their ideas are summarized at the close of each part of the report.[1]

The projected shape of the world in 2000, sketched in Part I, is by no means gloomy. But if the forecasts are correct, managers will face a very tough environment. Risks will be high, changes frequent and difficult to predict, external interference more intractable, and in spite of these difficulties the public will expect managerial results of a high order.

What kinds of managers will such a world require? Although

---

[1] Dr. Thomas L. Berg, Bronfman Fellow 1956–57, made especially valuable proposals, and would have been joint editor if our schedules had permitted.

no quantum shift is forecast, the analysis in Part II does point to significant qualitative changes. To function well in the predicted environment, managers will need more diplomatic ability, greater sensitivity to new values, skill in activating disenchanted employees, and a lot of agility in coping with new situations. The accent will be on sophisticated social skills, but with no diminution in technical abilities.

Surprisingly, the supply side of the picture is more likely to lead to conspicuous changes in the flow of managers, for reasons outlined in Part III. An oversupply of none-too-well-qualified aspiring managers will produce a scramble for jobs. Some candidates will resort to legal measures to obtain positions. Others will seek a more constructive "product differentiation" through advanced training and professional activities. A disgruntled fringe will drop out and complain. This competition for posts will place new burdens on employers and new demands on educators.

Two groups of proposed responses to these conditions are set forth in Part IV. Suggestions for education include a major advance in continuing education, professional certification, direct confrontation of value issues, political analysis, and meaningful training in not-for-profit management. If universities and colleges do not serve these and related needs, there is ample reason to believe other institutions will.

For companies the proposals described in Part IV include more deliberate training for change, rewarding "internal entrepreneurs," encouraging managers to participate in social planning, and explicit use of different management styles.

The report clearly implies that neither business leaders nor business educators can rest on their laurels. They may not like the proposals, but they cannot safely disregard the handwriting that is already visible on the wall.

PART I

SHAPE OF THE WORLD...
IN THE YEAR 2000

What kinds of managers we will need at the turn of the century depends on the state of the world at that time. If we could assume that economic, political, technological, and social affairs would remain substantially as at present, we could sketch—at least in major dimensions—the qualifications required. But the world is not standing still. Just as today's political map or telephone equipment may be grossly inadequate twenty years hence, the tasks of managing also are likely to differ.

To give us some feel for what the world may be like, Theodore J. Gordon outlines in the following paper an array of potential changes for the year 2000. Gordon is one of the world's top futurologists, and his views deserve thoughtful attention.

For present purposes—predicting future changes in the tasks of managers—a particular technological discovery or political event is not so important as the nature and rate of likely changes. In the jargon of the trade, a scenario will do; it will provide a base for our more specific analysis of vital managerial abilities that will be required in tomorrow's world.

by **THEODORE J. GORDON**[1]

A VIEW OF THE WORLD IN 2000

1. INTRODUCTION

The year 2000 is only as distant in the future as 1952 is in the past. For some of us 1952 is yet rather fresh in memory, and from this perspective, at least, 2000 looms as tomorrow. With the new century so close, can that world be very different from our own?

One measure of the magnitude of possible change in the next 24 years is the magnitude of change over the last such interval. In that time we saw, to name only a few of the more important developments: travel to the moon; enormous changes in foreign policy and the country's view of its role in world affairs; a doubling of world population; the advent of birth control pills and incredible changes in sex mores and family structure; huge growth in wealth, consumption, publication, education, travel, housing, and mobility; the fall of many governments, including our own; cold war changing to détente; genetic manipulation emerging from arcane theory and science fiction to laboratory reality; developments in solid-state physics leading to a technology that replaced the transistor and then went on to become microelectronics. And these are only changes at the surface. Changes in economics—even the perception of

[1] Prepared with the aid of Harold Becker, Lynne Heston, Robert Richmond, and Wayne Boucher—all members of The Futures Group.

economics—massive value changes, political changes in the role of society in politics: all of these are the essence of our time.

Various authors have tried to capture this essence in slogans or in titles of books. Toffler has called this the time of transience—a time of impermanence: our roots are not deep; we rent rather than own; few things are permanent. Harmon has called this the New Reformation, perhaps as important as the Old Reformation. He focuses on value change as the key element of our time. Revel calls this a peaceful revolution; to him the most important element of change is political. People are forging a new kind of relationship with their government—the notion of what it means to be a citizen is changing, not only in the United States, but throughout the world. Drucker calls this the age of discontinuity; he focuses on the rate of change itself. By almost any measure, change is accelerating, and that acceleration will make the future a different place, qualitatively, than our present time. Donald Michael calls this the unprepared society—unprepared for the onslaught of information from which there is no escape. Information descends on us from literally everywhere; the problem is not how to find out more, but rather how to turn it off and select only what is relevant. Bell sees us in a transition to post-industrialism. He argues that, in primitive societies, almost everyone had to work in agriculture. Then, as agricultural technology was improved and social organization was modified, fewer people were needed to produce the food required by society. Today, less than 5 percent of the U.S. labor force is involved in agriculture. A similar transition is apparently underway with respect to manufacturing; by 1985 fewer than one worker in four will be needed to manufacture all the goods we consume, store, or export. This will be the time of postindustrialism.

These, then, are the perspectives of change-in-progress: basic transitions are occurring in values, economics, demography, politics, and technology. Each author sees the characteristics of our time in terms of one or another of these dimensions, but they are all occurring simultaneously and all of the authors are right. The changes reinforce one another and interact in complex patterns, which we can only begin to perceive. Change, change in all of these dimensions, is the essence of our time.

These changes bring world problems—and opportunities—of unprecedented complexity and importance. Increasing agricultural production, distributing food, providing and conserving energy, finding alternatives to depleting nonrenewable resources, protecting the world's environment, stabilizing the internal and interacting economies of nations of the world, solving the problems implicit in the maldistribution of wealth, and—recognizing that all of these kinds of issues have in the past been causes for conflict—avoiding war: all of these prospects face us now and promise to intensify—instant by instant. They elude solution for many reasons: they are systemic—acting on one may intensify another; they require global perspective —attempts to correct the issues may require abandonment of chauvinism and unprecedented international cooperation; they are oriented to the long term—that is, they require giving priority to long-term considerations over short-run payoff.

2. THE SHAPE OF WORLD CRISES BY THE YEAR 2000[2]

World population is of the order of 4 billion people and is growing at the rate of about 2.2 percent per year. If this rate were to continue, world population would double in about 30 years. As Figure 1 shows, this is a new phenomenon; it is not an extension of the past. Over many, many centuries population growth rate was extremely slow. Then, in the Middle Ages, modern sanitation, the introduction of more advanced medical techniques, diminishing infant mortality, and other factors resulted in a population "take-off." Even if stringent birth control measures were to be quickly adopted by developing countries today, population growth rate would not be immediately curtailed; the future childbearing sector is already born. Almost no set of circumstances would keep world population below 6½ billion by the turn of the century.

This growth in population has enormous consequences for world affairs. If it were an objective, for example, to keep all measures of the human condition at current per capita levels, a population growth rate of 2.2 percent per year would imply that essentially everything that exists in the world today and all rates of production

[2] This section has been drawn from material prepared by The Futures Group for the National Aeronautics and Space Administration, *Project: Outlook for Space*, April 1975.

FIGURE 1.
World Population

THE GROWTH OF HUMAN NUMBERS

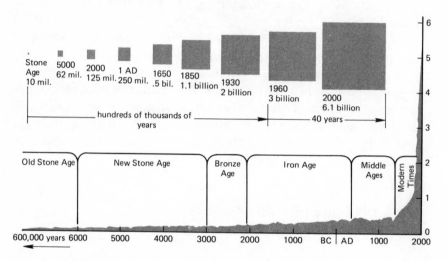

SOURCE: John McHale, *World Facts and Trends,* 2d ed. (New York: Collier Books, 1972), p. 34.

would have to double in about 30 years. The number of power plants, the number of schools, the number of books on library shelves, the amount of grain produced in a year, the amount of fresh water consumed, the number of houses: all of these would have to double.

Of course, this is a simplified view of things. It assumes the world is homogeneous, and the world is not. Population growth rate in developing countries is considerably higher than the world average; hence, to maintain per capita status quo in developing countries would require more than doubling in the next 35 years. Furthermore, the developing countries are not likely to be satisfied with goals that call for simply maintaining the per capital status quo; it is the objective of many developing countries to improve standards of living—and, necessarily, production and consumption—to emulate the currently developed countries. These aspirations may well be impossible to satisfy by any means, particularly in the presence of inexorable population growth. Therein lie the seeds for political turmoil.

We may have reached the "Malthusian" point by the year 2000. Essentially all of the arable land in the world will be in cultivation, and this land will produce enough to feed all people at about today's levels of consumption. Figure 2 illustrates this point. The horizontal line at 3.2 billion hectares represents the land available for agricultural production. The curve starts to drop off in the latter part of the century, because some of this land is rendered unavailable for food production by incursions of urbanization and roads. The lower line represents the amount of land required to feed everyone in the world, assuming people's diets maintain today's nutrition levels and that productivity per acre remains constant. The crossover between these two lines is just before the turn of the century. However, it is not necessary to assume that per acre productivity will remain constant; modern agricultural technology, the use of oceans, the introduction of new hybrid cereal varieties, new self-fertilizing plants, and

FIGURE 2
Arable land

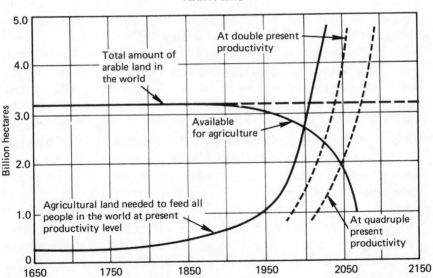

SOURCE: Donella H. Meadows et al., *The Limits to Growth* (New York: Universe Books, 1972).

hydroponics: all of these might add significantly to world food supplies. However, even if the effective production per acre could be
doubled, the crossover point would be moved out only two decades
or so; quadrupling would move the crossover out to the year 2050.
The effort implicit in doubling per acre productivity on a world basis
is enormous and, if these projections are to be believed, the world
has only a few decades to produce really meaningful results.

In developing countries, agricultural production and population growth have barely kept pace over the last decade; in the developed countries, per capita food consumption has grown faster than
population growth. This suggests that an important aspect of the
world food situation will be one of distribution, from high-income
countries to low-income countries. A recent study conducted at Iowa
State University indicates that, by the year 2000, the high-income
countries will have a surplus of between 225 and 385 million metric
tons. If low population growth rates are achieved in medium- and
low-income countries, this surplus will exceed their needs. However,
if population growth continues there at present rates, the surplus in
the high-income countries will be inadequate to meet their needs.[3]

Thus, in the affairs of nations over the next 25 years, food
must be a central issue. Will the developing countries be able to
produce the food they consume? If not, can the developed countries
of the world supply it? Will they be willing to?

In World War I, French battlefield physicians divided their
patients into three categories: those who would clearly survive without medical attention, those who would die even with medical attention, and those who would survive but only with medical attention.
This system of division was known as "triage." The physicians, of
course, devoted their full attention to the third category of patients.
Today, people are seriously considering the possibility that developed countries view the impoverished developing countries in the
same way—that is, identify those who will survive with aid. Viewing
triage in the context of world food problems, some nations will
undergo a transition to self-sufficiency with or without aid. Other
nations, given assistance, may reach self-sufficiency. However, the
third category includes countries whose population growth rates are

---

[3] *World Food Production, Demand, and Trade* (Ames, Iowa: Iowa State
University Press, 1973).

so high and whose food production capacity is so precarious that aid would not be catalytic in attaining self-sufficiency.[4] The notion of triage as applied to the world food situation is grim, suggesting the nature of the hard choices that must be faced by the developed countries in the next few decades.

Both the developed and the developing countries have been getting richer in terms of their annual income (it is also true within the United States: both the poor and the nonpoor are getting richer). This is a happy situation. But in the world as a whole the rate of increase of annual GNP and GNP per capita is greater in the developed countries than in the developing countries; hence the gap in income is growing. And the gap is appreciable. Eighty percent of the world's population lives in countries that generate only about 15 percent of the world's annual product. By the turn of the century, assuming present trends continue, the 85 percent of the world's population living in the poorer countries will generate only about 12 percent of the world's annual product.

In an attempt to change this situation the United Nations began "The Decade of Development" in 1960. However, its strategies were only partially successful, and the development rate of the poorer countries remained relatively low.

Wealth is not equivalent to income; it can be measured in terms of aggregated capital or natural endowment. Wealth represents the potential for future income. While aggregated capital clearly is concentrated in the developed countries, natural resources are more homogeneously distributed. As the Middle East situation demonstrated, when a few nations control a resource, they can readily exert monopolistic power. Hence, as the supply of certain materials grows short, the definition of which countries are "have" and which are "have-not" nations will change.

In the years to come the United States will not become a have-not nation, but it will rely more heavily on other nations for necessary materials. By the year 2000, under the assumption of continued economic growth in the United States, more than 90 percent of all the chromium, copper, tin, titanium, platinum, beryllium,

[4] William Paddock and Paul Paddock, *Famine—1975!* (Boston: Little, Brown & Co. 1967); and Paul R. Ehrlich and Ann H. Ehrlich, *Population, Resources, Environment: Issues in Human Ecology,* 2nd ed. (San Francisco: W. H. Freeman & Company, 1972).

aluminum, and fluorine the country consumes will have to be imported.

A paradigm for forecasting future OPEC-like situations might be to identify key materials industrial nations use that are concentrated in a few other nations that could be linked politically. It is unlikely that nations that control minerals can exert the same level of pressure on the United States as did OPEC (simply because the U.S. economy is less dependent on minerals than on petroleum); nevertheless, the world already has several examples of mineral cartel actions. Morocco, Tunisia, Senegal, and Algeria recently agreed to raise the price of phosphate rock; this led to increases in the price of fertilizer and detergent. The suppliers of bauxite, the principal raw material used in aluminum production, have met several times and have agreed on price-setting strategies. Producers of mercury met in 1974 to agree on pricing principles, and other organizations such as the International Tin Council and the Intergovernment Council of Copper Exporting Countries already exist. These and other formal and informal groupings of exporting nations can be expected to set prices on the world market.

The rising world demand for raw materials is based on two factors: the number of people in the world is increasing and per capita consumption is increasing. As mentioned earlier, world population will soon double. Concurrently, following past trends, per capita mineral consumption will increase by a factor of 4. Therefore, combining these two forces in the next 30 years the world as a whole may increase its mineral consumption by a factor of 8 or so. Failure to achieve this growth would mean that developing countries would not be able to achieve current economic goals, an outcome that seems likely. Furthermore, the United States is likely to find itself in growing competition for an increasingly inadequate supply of many mineral resources.

Of all the minerals the United States imports, perhaps petroleum is the most important. The 1973–1974 Arab oil embargo vividly demonstrated the need for an ordering of national energy priorities and policies. The major questions are: To what degree need we rely on foreign sources of energy? How will supply and demand come into balance? To what extent can domestic supply be stimulated and demand restrained? To what degree will lifestyle changes be required to bring about supply/demand balance?

Clearly, at least for the next 20 years, energy will be more costly than in the past[5] and is likely to be in short supply in some sectors of the United States, causing changes in social values and economic conditions. The basic reasons are:

1. Energy demand is expected to increase at about the rate of 3.6 percent per year from 1970–1980.

2. Domestic crude oil production appears to have peaked in 1971. Optimistic projections (which include the North Slope) are for domestic crude oil production to slowly decline over the next 15 years.

3. There have been delays in building nuclear power plants and bringing them to full power production due to diminished demand for electrical energy, environmental concerns, and certain engineering difficulties.

4. Recent environmental laws prohibiting the burning of high-sulfur coal place an extra burden on oil and natural gas usage.

5. Environmental pressure has delayed the construction of oil refineries and other energy-related facilities.

One of the most important consequences of these trends is the need to increase petroleum importation. Total demand can be forecasted on the basis of assumed continuing growth of the U.S. economy and a continuation of current lifestyles. The supply of oil, gas, coal, hydroelectric energy, and nuclear sources can be estimated with fair certainty over the near term. Comparing domestic supply with anticipated demand indicates a continuing and probably growing gap. There are very few ways in which this gap can be closed:

1. Increasing amounts of petroleum can be imported.

2. Policies can be established and technologies introduced in an effort to increase domestic supply.

3. Policies can be established and technologies introduced in an effort to reduce consumption.

[5] Energy Policy Project of the Ford Foundation Report, *A Time to Choose—America's Energy Future* (Cambridge, Mass.: Ballinger Publishing Co., 1973).

The prospect of importing ever-increasing amounts of petroleum is disturbing for several reasons. It implies growing dependence on foreign nations for material that is intimately bound to America's economy and lifestyle. Furthermore, because of high cost, it leads inevitably to an unfavorable balance of trade. Finally, the national security aspects of a situation in which the United States must continually import a major portion of its fuel cannot be overlooked.

It does not appear that new energy technology can provide much help during the 1980s. The nation is rich in coal, and this energy source will be a major factor in meeting demand: production of coal could be approximately doubled during the next 15 to 20 years. However, there are real limits on coal production and utilization, including availability of manpower; environmental considerations, particularly those associated with strip-mining and the sulfur content of coal; and the safety and health of the workers involved in mining operations.

Nuclear power is useful only in producing electricity. The rate of growth of demand for electricity was sharply reduced after the oil embargo as a result of increasing electricity prices and public energy awareness. The changing demand for electricity led to the cancellation of orders for many nuclear plants and a delay in the initiation of construction of many others. Therefore, it is likely that conventional nuclear power will not furnish as much energy as originally anticipated by the turn of the century.

More exotic technologies, such as solar energy, geothermal power, and fusion, will require research and pilot plant operation before they can be counted on to produce appreciable amounts of power. At best, solar and geothermal energy may begin to make a substantial contribution in the 1990s; fusion power will probably not be a significant source before the mid- to late 1990s, or perhaps even after the turn of the century.

Almost all of the socioeconomic-political issues on the horizon seem to be politically destabilizing: overpopulation, shortage of food, cartelism, terrorism, and pressures to redistribute wealth to developing countries. War is possible. War is conceivable. Even nuclear war. This issue, unique in our times, is clearly among the most difficult and dangerous that nations of the world have ever faced. It is unique because of the high level of killing potential now stored in weapons; it is difficult because disarming, even arms limitation in some instances, is seen as counter to national interests. War is increasingly dangerous for three reasons. First, more nations, and even groups within nations, are going to have vastly increased killing potential in the near future. Second, new, inexpensive, easy-to-conceal weapons are at hand. Finally, the danger stems from the apparently inevitable clashes between nations over food, minerals, energy, and the distribution of wealth.

There is, of course, great difficulty in assembling reliable figures on military expenditures throughout the world. Nevertheless, various organizations within the United Nations and peace institutes throughout the world have gleaned enough data to form an idea of the massive world scope of military spending:

1. On a worldwide basis, military expenditures have been increasing about 6 percent per year, in constant dollars, since 1950.

2. The level of military budgets for 1970 totaled $200 billion.

3. Since military expenditures, on the average, are growing faster than either world GNP or world population, the absolute burden and per capita burden are both increasing.

4. As an example of the size of the military enterprise, in 1967 military costs were 7 percent of the world GNP—equal to the total annual income of one billion people living in Latin America, Southeast Asia, and the Middle East. The manpower in military service totals some 50 million people.

5. World military expenditures exceed expenditures for public education, public health, and foreign aid; public education amounted to about 70 percent of military expenditures, public health about 30 percent, and foreign economic aid, about 6 percent.

6. In the United States, somewhat less than 10 percent of the gross national product has been devoted to military spending.

7. In the late 1960s the developing countries accounted for only 11 percent of the world's total military expenditures: $8 per capita versus $170 per capita in the developed countries. In absolute terms their spending averaged 4 percent of gross national product versus 8 percent in the developed countries.

8. Yet even in the developing countries, military expenditures

far exceed expenditures for public education and public health (in 1966, $17 billion for the armed forces, $11 billion for public education, and $5 billion for public health).[6]

9. In real terms, military expenditures in developed countries peaked in 1968, but the growth rate of military spending in developing countries has increased sharply. Since 1961, military spending in 93 developing nations has more than doubled.[7]

Some nations are carrying an incredible per capita burden to support their military expenditures. Although their per capita GNP was under $200 in 1970, Egypt, the Sudan, China, Burma, and the Somali Republic all had military expenditures amounting to more than 50 percent of the GNP. At the other extreme, Luxembourg had a per capita GNP of $3000 and yet its military expenditures were below 1 percent of the GNP of that country.

In thinking about the possibility of war, consider the following: the number of nuclear weapons around the world is huge; the United States has over 30,000 located within the United States, at sea, and in foreign countries. Of these, 8500 are strategic and 22,000 tactical. The Soviet Union has approximately 5500 nuclear weapons, of which 3000 are tactical. The total explosive force available in nuclear weapons is somewhat more than 50,000 megatons—this is equivalent to 15 tons of TNT for each person in the world. Six nations today have exploded nuclear weapons; by the turn of century that number may double. New members of the "club" may include: Israel, Egypt, Argentina, Brazil, Pakistan, South Africa, and Spain. SALT has not produced arms reduction—rather, it has sanctioned an increase in the level of armament. Furthermore, the possible introduction of new weapons such as submarine-launched cruise missiles has confounded SALT. Proliferation of new weapons seems quite likely. Most nations in the world believe that nuclear weapons can be equated to greater security. In addition, there is a general expectation that nuclear explosives will prove useful for peaceful

[6] Archibald S. Alexander, "The Cost of World Armaments," *Scientific American,* October 1969, pp. 21–27.

[7] *World Military Expenditures, 1971,* U.S. Arms Control and Disarmament Agency, July 1972.

purposes. Finally, the expanding use of nuclear-generated power facilities makes available, through the reprocessing cycle, enriched uranium that can be used in weapons. By 1980 at least 30 countries will have built nuclear power reactors.

While nuclear weapons are most visible, a host of other ugly weapons exist, including chemical weapons—incapacitants, nerve gas, blister agents, and riot control drugs; binary chemical weapons; biological weapons—now banned by treaty; and a new product of research, artificial viruses.

The Preamble to the Charter of the United Nations reads in part:

> We the peoples of the United Nations, determined to save succeeding generations from the scourge of war, which twice in our lifetime has brought untold sorrow to mankind, and to reaffirm faith in fundamental human rights, in the dignity and worth of the human person, ... and of nations large and small ... to promote social progress ... to practice tolerance ... to maintain international peace ... and resolve to combine our efforts to accomplish these aims.

We are enormously distant from this ideal. By the turn of the century, to avoid the catastrophe of war, nations of the world must achieve realistic arms limitations, disarm if at all possible, and stabilize and diffuse the issues that can lead to war.

3. THE SHAPE OF TECHNOLOGY

Science and technology interact strongly with all of these world problems. Future scientific and technological developments could help solve—or intensify—most of these issues. Recognizing that advancing science and technology sometimes have imposed significant social and human costs, intellectual criticism of both science and technology has been mounting. The view that technology can continue to solve problems is challenged; critics believe that further technological development may bring a net social loss. Whether in response to or leading this criticism, public attitudes toward science and technology have been changing as well.

In fact, some scientific and technological developments of the recent past have been threatening and have had obvious deleterious consequences. There are prospects for more such inventions in the years immediately ahead. It should not be surprising that science occasionally produces intrinsically threatening developments, because its structure is asocial; that is, social need is not a major determinant of the direction of research.

Yet, despite the rise of an intellectual antitechnology movement, and a similar popular sentiment, and despite the odious technologies of the past, the need for innovative contributions from the basic and applied sciences and from the physical and social technologies has never been greater. Nevertheless, the institutional difficulties that inhibit these contributions are enormous. If they could be overcome to some extent, science and technology could make more important contributions to the solution of world problems and to improvements in the state of man. We must work to that end.

When we examine current technology-in-progress, two important major themes emerge: miniaturized electronics and the new biology. The microelectronics revolution, perhaps most visible in the emergence of miniaturized electronic calculators, springs from several key inventions. The field effect, in which the lateral conduction within a crystal is controlled by an electric field applied at right angles, was described as early as 1930 by Julius E. Lilienfeld, who patented the concept in 1935. Walter Schottky's work in rectification, which occurs at the junction of a metal and a semiconductor, led directly to the invention of a point-contact transistor in 1947 by William B. Shockley, John Bardeen, and Walter Brattain. In 1953 George C. Dacey and Ian M. Ross built a field-effect transistor using concepts published earlier by Shockley. This work led to a family of devices, small compared to the vacuum tube, that could be used in rather conventional circuits requiring various other components, such as resistors, capacitors, and diodes. The microelectronics revolution really begain in 1960 when techniques were invented to "integrate" circuits—that is, to combine most of the elements of the circuit on a single-crystal silicate wafer. Early integrated circuits involved a few dozen components per chip and measured a few millimeters on a side. By the mid-1970s the number of elements per chip was of the order of tens of thousands, and by the mid-1980s chips of the order of a million components will not be unusual.

As the packing densities increased, the costs dropped. The first integrated circuits each cost about one dollar. Today, as fabrication skills have developed, the cost has dropped to about 1 cent per component. By the mid-1980s costs will drop two orders of magnitude: .001 cent per component.

With many of the old constraints of cost, size, and complexity now effectively removed, almost anything electronically imaginable is possible. The electronic calculator boom of the 1970s was made possible through the use of MOS circuitry. Electromechanical units had cost about $1000. Once large-scale integrated circuits were introduced, the price dropped from hundreds of dollars to $50 or even less.

Microelectronics will be pervasive. In health and health delivery systems, they will contribute to new kinds of diagnostic techniques, to the development of supple prosthetics, and even to therapeutics.

Military uses of large-scale integrated circuitry will accelerate the field. Military strength is determined not only by counts of weapons and men, but by the speed with which they can be deployed, the subtlety of the levels of response, the ability to collect and convey information from field to command and from command to field, the accuracy and precision of fire control, and, most important of all, the ease with which sophisticated equipment can be used by simple men. All of these are electronic attributes; microelectronics can make the difference between an advanced military force and an archaic one.

Among military applications are remote pilotless bombers, advanced means of target recognition, accurate identification of electronic "signatures," new kinds of remote sensors, electronic or chemical methods to "label" friends and enemies, robot soldiers, and logistics.

This new technology will play a major role in future communications and transportation. Automobiles, for example, will become safer and more convenient as the result of the use of microelectronic systems. Automobiles will have digital display instrumentation that can present on command information about trip speed, fuel consumption, incipient malfunctions, etc. In addition, on-board electronic devices will meter fuel injection for fuel economy and improvements of the order of 20 percent. Computers will manage the braking system to prevent skids, and very simple radarlike devices will warn of impending collisions.

Businesses will have a battery of devices made possible only by microelectronics. Noiseless typewriters, facsimile, automated data correspondence files, access to various sorts of data banks, interoffice electronic communications, and electronic composing and reprographic equipment are all possible.

The biological revolution is apt to be more important and more pervasive than the electronic. In 1953 Francis Crick, Maurice Wilkins, and James Watson defined the double-helix structure of the DNA molecule. They proposed that each strand of this double helix was composed of a sequence of amino acids and that the sequence itself was the "genetic code." In other words, the placement of specific submolecules along the chain determined the genetic properties of the cell. This notion, rapidly accepted by geneticists, triggered a large-scale search to identify the specific genetic traits associated with specific sequences of molecules on the chain.

This research has moved very fast. By early 1975 experiments had been performed in which genetic information had been transferred from one species to another. The technique by which this experiment was accomplished has the potential for creating novel, self-replicating microorganisms. Clearly, such a possibility has ambivalent implications: while these experiments can provide fundamental information on genetic processes and possibly result in the introduction of favorable genetic characteristics into plants and animals, they could also create, through accident or purpose of manipulation, organisms capable of promoting specific diseases, including cancer, or pathenogenic toxins.

The scientists involved in this research recognized the dual implication of this technology and established a voluntary moratorium on certain types of recombinant DNA research. At Asilomar in Februrary 1975, over 140 scientists from 17 countries met to discuss their self-imposed regulations. Inherent in the scientists' concern with the potential biohazards of recombinant DNA were several basic value issues concerning the relations between science and society. In forming, deciding upon, and implementing basic ethical restraints on research, these scientists were enacting one of the few cases in which, as Paul Berg stated, "anyone has to stop and think about an experiment in terms of its social impact and potential hazard." More precise and stringent research guidelines have been drafted by a committee of the National Institutes of Health. This research direction has now been reinstated under these guidelines.

What could it mean? At the simple end is the ability to create new kinds of plant varieties, to create mutations to order. One very important line of research is the transfer of the genetic property of certain plants, legumes, to interact symbiotically with micro-organisms in the soil to fix nitrogen from the atmosphere. This process is essentially self-fertilization, and if it can be transferred to plants such as wheat or corn, food productivity might be increased tremendously. This line of genetic research will undoubtedly be extended to human beings. The first application might well be to attempt to eliminate genetically transmitted diseases such as PKU and Mongolism. Many other diseases are believed to have genetic origins, such as diabetes, heart disease, cancer, and perhaps even aging itself. Greater understanding of the genetic process may eventually lead to the creation of food factories in which, through cloning, cells replicate themselves in order to produce protein that can be consumed directly by human beings. This would be the first instance, in all of civilization, in which nonnatural food was manufactured by society for human consumption.

The potential is indeed great.

4. THE SHAPE OF CHANGE IN AMERICA BY THE YEAR 2000[8]

Many socioeconomic trends in America are moving in favorable directions. If we could have forecasted these trends 20 years ago, we might have been called hopelessly idealistic and optimistic. Nevertheless, today these trends are real.

　　1. Life expectancy at birth in the United States has risen from about 50 years at the turn of the century to a little over 70 years at present.

　　2. Death from heart disease has fallen from slightly under 300 per 100,000 population in 1950 to about 250 per 100,000 at the present.

[8] Some of the following material is derived from T. Gordon and W. Boucher, *Some Thoughts on the Future* (Glastonbury, Conn.: The Futures Group, May 1975).

3. While infant mortality rates for Negroes and other races in the United States are considerably higher than infant mortality rates for whites, great progress has been achieved; in 1940 nonwhite infant mortality dropped to 80 deaths per 100,000 live births; by 1970 this number had dropped to 30 deaths per 100,000; and the trend is rapidly approaching the national average of about 20 deaths per 100,000 live births.

4. Numbers of resident patients in mental hospitals have declined, primarily as a result of the use of major tranquilizers. In 1955 there were over 500,000 resident patients in mental hospitals; the total now is about 250,000. People who would formerly have been institutionalized can now lead relatively normal lives in society.

5. Drop-out rates in schools are diminishing; in 1924 only about 30 percent of the children who finished fifth grade also finished high school; by 1972 the number had risen to just under 80 percent.

6. Many more people in our country are going to college; in 1957 total enrollment in institutions of higher education was about 3.5 million; by 1971 the total was over 9 million. In 1940 about 4.6 percent of all people over 25 years of age had completed four years of college; by 1972 this number had risen to 12 percent.

7. Over the last few decades women have entered the labor force at unprecedented rates: in 1948 only about 17 million women participated in the labor force; by 1972 this number had about doubled. During the same period the number of men in the labor force increased by only about 25 percent.

8. Families in America are becoming more affluent: in terms of constant 1971 dollars, median family income in 1947 was $5500; by 1971 the median family income was $10,285.

9. Real income, that is, buying power of the individual, increased by about 43 percent in the period from 1960–1973. Only one nation increased more than that in the same period —Japan. Per capita income in the United States is still considerably greater than in Japan.

10. Although food prices have increased recently, they represent a steadily diminishing portion of personal disposable in-

come: in 1947 food represented almost 32 percent of personal consumption expenditures; in 1972 food purchases required less than 20 percent.

11. In 1959 about 21 percent of all of U.S. families were below the poverty level; by 1971 this number was less than 11 percent.

12. Affluence can be measured in another dimension as well: average weekly hours worked. In 1943 the average length of the work week was 48 hours; by 1972 it had dropped to 39 hours.

13. The percentage of substandard housing units has been steadily dropping: in 1940, 48 percent of all housing units were classed as substandard—that is, they were dilapidated or lacked some or all plumbing. By 1970 this number had diminished to 7.4 percent.

14. By 1972 only 1.5 percent of all married couples had not established their own households.

15. Fertility rates have fallen to very low levels—below 75 births per 1000 women of childbearing age. At this rate, soon after the turn of the century we can expect the size of the population of the United States to stabilize at a level somewhat below 300 million.

16. On the world scene, great progress has been made in food production. During the last two decades food production grew at about 218 percent annually in both developing and developed countries, exceeding the 2 percent annual growth rate in population. Therefore, on the average, the 3.8 billion people of the world in 1973 had about 20 percent more to eat per person than the 2.7 billion living 20 years earlier. (The world food problem stems, at least partially, from the fact that population growth rate in developing countries is essentially equal to the growth of agricultural production; thus the great increases in productive capacity have not yielded any per capita gains.)

17. The United States is one of the few nations of the world that can raise enough grain to satisfy its own needs and still have appreciable exports—and this is accomplished with less than 4 percent of our labor force.

18. Certainly energy availability has been an important concern—but conservation measures and public awareness seem to be reducing demand. In many parts of the country electricity demand has leveled off; because of lower highway speeds, deaths due to accidents have diminished considerably; and the level of awareness of the intimate relationship between our economy and energy availability is much more widespread.

19. Hard drug use is down; more minority people have been elected to office than ever before; laws prohibiting discrimination on the basis of race or sex are on the books and seem to be having good effect; the physical environment is improving in many places; rock music is quieter now than in the last decade; the economy seems to be headed for a turnaround; and the longest war of the twentieth century has ended.

It would be grossly unjustified to paint this optimistic picture without recognizing that these same statistics might convey entirely different meanings to other people; what is seen as good by one may be seen as odious by another. Furthermore, these statistics mask subtrends that in themselves may not be as promising or desirable as the overall trend itself; for example, while the number of women in the labor force is increasing, there is still a great disparity in salaries paid to women for jobs similiar to those performed by men. There remain continuing and intransigent biases against women and racial minorities. Nevertheless, the positive trends suggest that important progress has been made in our country toward what most of us would consider a better life.

Against this background we must recognize that perhaps even more significant changes are taking place in the United States today. For several decades the United States has experienced a long-term downward trend of birth rate, and as a result the population has been growing older. The downward trend was interrupted by the post-World War II baby boom, but the decline in birth rate since the latter part of the 1950s has caused the proportion of the population in childhood years to become smaller once again. (See Figure 3.)

If birth rate remains low, population in the United States will stabilize at roughly 250 million by the year 2020 (Figure 4). That is, of course, significant, but it may be even more important to mention that low birth rate and stabilization of the population also imply

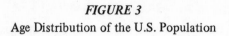

FIGURE 3

Age Distribution of the U.S. Population

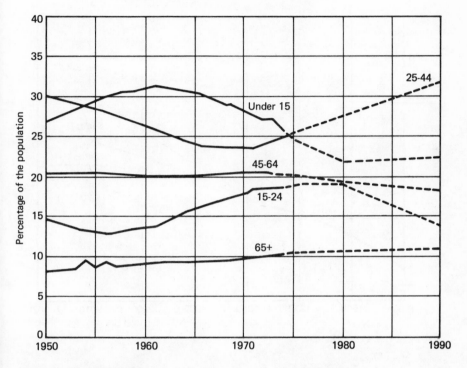

SOURCE OF HISTORICAL DATA: U.S. Bureau of the Census, *Current Population Reports,*
Series P-25, Nos. 311 and 519.
SOURCE OF PROJECTION: U.S. Bureau of the Census, Series E.

markedly changing age distribution. Figure 5 portrays the percentage
growth in population of various age cohorts in the decade between
1975 and 1985. The "bump" in the age group between 25 and 44
represents the post-World War II baby boom babies. Fifteen years
earlier this bulge extended from age 10 through 30 and helps explain,
at least in part, our prior emphasis on youth. With the aging of these
people, emphasis naturally shifts to issues associated with family
formation. The increase of children between the ages of 0 and 4
represents the children of the people now reaching family formation
years. The dip in the 10- through 19-year age group helps explain
why schools currently are uncrowded.

   One can carry this sort of age-distribution chart further into

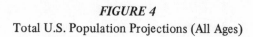

FIGURE 4
Total U.S. Population Projections (All Ages)

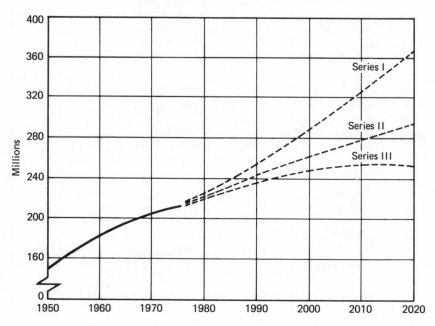

SOURCE: U.S. Census Bureau.

the future. In the interval between 1985 and 1995 there is likely to be an increasing emphasis on problems of the aged. In that interval the number of people at or nearing retirement age will be growing faster than the age groups that comprise the labor force. There will undoubtedly be questions of viability of pension funds and Social Security mechanisms.

The percentage of women in the labor force will rise gradually, but the most drastic changes in sex composition are behind us. The most significant change will be the increase in the number of working women with young children. Employment by government and the service sector, as compared with employment by the goods-producing industries, will increase. Growth in professional and managerial jobs will continue to outpace other categories and will include more women.

There probably will be a trend toward somewhat greater stabil-

FIGURE 5
Demographic Growth Patterns in the United States
by Age Groups, 1975–1985, Series II

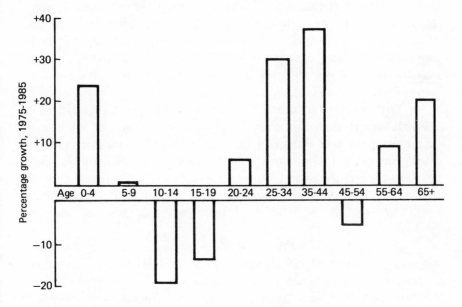

SOURCE: U.S. Bureau of the Census, *Current Population Reports,* Series P-25, No. 601, "Projections of the Population of the United States: 1975 to 2050" (Washington, D.C.: U.S. Government Printing Office, 1975), Table 8, pp. 67, 77.

ity of employment as more jobs are located in the government and service sectors. Employee unions and associations will show greatest growth in the nonmanufacturing sector, particularly among government workers. As long as inflation continues at a high rate, emphasis on collective bargaining will probably be on higher wages rather than on increased fringe benefits.

The educational level of the labor force will continue to rise. By 1990 fully 40 percent of the labor force will have attended one or more years of college (as opposed to about 25 percent currently). Twenty percent of the labor force will have had four years or more of college (compared to about 15 percent currently). There will be an increasing oversupply of educated young people, and many college graduates will have to accept lower-level jobs than they had expected. Job requirements will accordingly be raised.

It will be difficult to increase the productivity of the labor force enough to keep pace with labor-cost increases. Again, this can be attributed to the growth in the nongoods-producing and government sectors of the economy, where productivity increases are more difficult to attain but where wage levels and employee benefits continue to rise. In the near term at least, productivity is unlikely to be impaired by major changes in work attitudes, although employers may need to adjust to meet the heightened rights and social consciousness of young employees.

With respect to the U.S. economy, the simultaneous and inherently contradictory needs to control inflation and to control unemployment will remain major political and economic problems during the remainder of the 1970s. There seems to be little chance of a 1930s-type depression because of the built-in stabilizers, such as Social Security, welfare payments, and unemployment compensation, although the high level of unemployment will subside only gradually.

Americans will continue to view owning their own home as a major goal and as an effective way to increase their net worth. The underlying long-term demand for housing will be up and will be bolstered by the high rate of new household formation in the young adult age group. However, the form of housing may change drastically and will probably include mobile homes, high-rise, and "no-frills" housing. The increased number of retirees will be accommodated by lower-cost, smaller units that require little or no maintenance by the owner. New methods of financing, such as variable-rate mortgages, will be devised to deal with the prevailing credit climate.

The amount of time spent on leisure and recreation will continue to increase. Participation in recreational activities will continue to have high income elasticity.

Thus, in the next 25 years or so, average age in the United States will increase. Emphasis will be on problems of the aged and retiring rather than of youth. The good life will still be sought and largely achieved, problems of the economy and employment notwithstanding.

Besides the world crises, developments in technology, and changes in America we have discussed, other trends promise to make the world at the turn of the century different from any we have ever known before. Here are some of the trends that overlie the issues, interact with them, and will shape their consequences:

1. More and more often questions about growth are being raised. Clearly, in a bounded system, exponential growth reaches limits. Some argue that as we approach these limts, the situation must become traumatic, bringing an abrupt end to rising expectations, revising institutions, causing conflict and much human suffering.

2. Values are in transition. New attitudes are clearly developing with respect to the environment, interpersonal relations, the family, institutional authority, and welfare and "entitlements" of citizens. There is every indication that some of these value changes will be lasting and will affect the way people interact with one another and with the institutions to which they lend their power.

3. Almost all of the trends discussed have certain consequences in common, including the fact that policies directed toward their solution will be costly to implement, inflationary, and potentially politically destabilizing.

4. Perhaps most important of all, there is a growing recognition that problems and their solutions cannot be viewed in isolation; rather they are elements of a complex system that interacts across national boundaries and organizations and across subsystem elements. A property of complex systems is that corrective actions sometimes produce unexpected consequences—both counterintuitive results and reactions in other parts of the system. Attempting to cure aspects of the environmental problem can have impacts on energy availability; attempting to improve agricultural output can have deleterious consequences for the environment. This interrelatedness is becoming part of the consciousness, and conscience, of planning.

These, then, are some of the threads in the fabric of change. Some trends suggest that many of the goals of the past decades are being achieved or at least substantially approached. Others portend a growing confluence of issues of enormous proportions: population growth; its concomitant pressures on the world's ecology; the problems of food and agriculture; the expanding world need for energy and raw materials. And all of them lead to the suggestion that massive, fundamental value and institutional changes are in progress, both as a result and as a cause.

Our image of the future will shape our reactions, our initiatives. If we dream of doom, we embrace it. If we imagine that old Disjointed Incrementalism will somehow put things right, we dream of times not long past, when we could indulge the luxury of dealing with one issue at a time; we dream the dream of slow decline, in which the maturity of old age may well be indistinguishable from senility. But if we dream not merely of enduring, but of prevailing, we have the chance of finding opportunities in threats, understanding in perplexity. Therein lie our choices—and the character of the age that will be our legacy.

EMERGING CONTOURS
AFFECTING MANAGEMENT

The picture Gordon paints is exciting, sobering, challenging. The full implications of the strains in food and energy redistribution, income gaps, new biological and electronic technology, a more aged population, and other developments Gordon sketches take time to grasp. And yet in the allotted pages he necessarily omitted additional forces to which managers have to respond. Several of these are emphasized in the Bronfman Fellows' comments on Gordon's paper.

The flagging of strains is tantalizing. We want to know more. What can and should be done? What is the probable response to such moves? Because of the interrelatedness of politics and economics, social values and resource allocations, and the like, action taken on one front will ease or complicate action on other problems. This makes specific forecasts for ten to twenty years ahead hazardous.

While specific forecasts may be necessary for particular decisions—such as the building of a power dam—a program for manager development can be launched on more general (and predictable) premises. The *nature* of managerial problems at the turn of the century, in contrast to specific problems, will provide an adequate basis for today's moves. Our prime concern is initiating now the selection, training, motivation, and organizational practices that will assure a flow of future managers qualified to deal with tomorrow's challenges. And we can foresee with confidence many of the characteristics of those challenges.

Here is a list of seven features of the world ahead that will affect significantly the kind of managers needed.

1. Change—frequent change on diverse fronts. Clearly the tensions outlined by Gordon, the restlessness throughout the world, our improved communication, a disregard for established social order, coupled with a capability to move mountains, will sustain the rate of change we are already experiencing. For the manager, both private and public, adaptability will be the price of survival and anticipating changes the key to eminence.

2. Extension of sophisticated technology. We have learned to expect new products and to seek change for change's sake. And overall the pace is still rising. Many of the newer technologies, such as the miniature electronics and manipulative biology noted by Gordon, call for great sophistication. This appears to be leading to a breakdown of traditional industry boundaries—for example, in finance as well as communications—and to new forms of competition. For developing nations, the technological gap is becoming incomprehensible.

3. Sharp shifts in resource allocations and political power as new "limits on growth" surface. Most of the recognized "limits" on growth—energy, food, water, air—can be overcome at least into the next century. But the resources required, even with improved technology, are staggering. This forebodes shifts of capital and equipment away from traditional uses for modest gains in per capita output. Government interference and subsidy will be irresistible. Moreover, as scarcities tighten, dependence on foreign supplies will increase, and this in turn will sharply alter the political bargaining position of many nations. Some individual companies will prosper while others wither.

4. Growth in the service sector—both governmental and private. In terms of percentage of employment, the movement away from agriculture into industry and now away from industry into intangible services is well established. This shift will continue. Since managing in government and in other service organizations differs from managing the production and distribution of physical products, the rising importance of intangibles calls for innovative techniques. Improvements in productivity are especially elusive.

5. Greater expectations about management results. In addition to dealing with the preceding forces, managers will be expected by the public to conduct their enterprises so as to (a) meet rising and changing views on environmental protection, urban renewal, and other social concerns and (b) at the same time provide jobs that are challenging, stable, tailored to individual needs, and demonstrably free of discrimination. If results fail to meet expectations, some people will turn to governmental action, but this will merely bring pressure on managers from another source.

6. More group confrontations. Resort to individual bargaining appears to be waning. Increasingly, when some change is sought, a group is formed. Labor unions, consumer groups, the Sierra Club, neighborhood organizations, investor associations, minority clubs, Women's Liberation—all present their particular demands. The variety of techniques of harassment is growing. By the year 2000 some additional ground-rules for group confrontations will undoubtedly have been written; but the difficulty of enforcing such rules relating to labor unions—both in the United States and abroad—suggests that organized group pressure will rise as a potent instrument.

7. More government checks and supports. An array of forces conspire to raise government participation in business affairs. Inflation and unemployment will still hound us in 2000. Supports for critical resources will bring associated regulation. International operations will be more closely supervised. Protections of health, environment, minorities, investors, civil liberties, and a host of other worthy causes will be written into law. Business ethics and especially the exercise of power by large corporations will be further circumscribed. Although occasional withdrawal can be expected, overall we will continue the habit of turning to federal, state, and local governments to help build a better society.

Such is the world that managers will confront at the turn of the century. Frequent change, more dependence on sophisticated technology, resource limitations leading to shifts in political power, growing importance of intangible service—all will complicate the tasks of managing. At the same time the public's expectations of results, the criteria managers will be expected to meet, will escalate. And to add salt to the wounds, managers must achieve these results while finding new ways to deal with group confrontations and governmental interference.

This is an incomplete picture, to be sure, but the contours are clear enough to provide trenchant guidance to current managerial development.

PART II

CHARACTERISTICS of MANAGERS . . .
NEEDED iN THE YEAR 2000

Managing in the year 2000 will be a tough job. The task will be more complex, the tensions greater, the expected results higher, and the constraints more burdensome—as we have just seen in Part I. Now, to focus more sharply on supplying managers who will be competent to deal with such conditions, we turn to the characteristics of people needed for that challenging job.

Marvin Bower outlines in the following paper the personal qualities he believes will be especially useful. He centers on "business leadership" and explains the broad meaning he attaches to that term. In his long and highly successful consulting career, Bower has observed intimately many senior company executives; probably more than any other living person he has shared the hopes and the frustrations of chief executive officers as they perceived their staffing problems. His direct, uncluttered manner of speech and writing belie the range of experience from which he draws his conclusions.

Bower stresses fundamentals. In analyzing his paper our panelists, the Bronfman Fellows, did not seriously disagree, but they felt that several of the environmental pressures will place a premium in the future on particular attributes. These points of elaboration will be reviewed following Bower's basic framework.

CHARACTERISTICS OF MANAGER

Media in the Year 2000

by **MARVIN BOWER**

CORPORATE LEADERS FOR THE YEAR 2000

One of the cliches of corporate planning calls for "controlling the future." If that notion has any validity at all, it probably is found in the feasibility of the individual corporation's providing its leaders for the year 2000. However, if that objective is to be achieved by promotion from within (as it should be), a definite company program should be underway now or should be started soon. It is really a matter of management *will,* now and in the future, whether a firm's leaders will be ready in the year 2000.[1]

Processes Simple and Well Known

The present leaders of any corporation can begin to provide its leaders for a quarter century ahead by establishing a program made up of simple and well-known personnel processes for people now alive or even now on the corporate payroll.

Therefore, if the individual corporation is to provide the best possible leadership for the year 2000, the leaders of *today* and of the intervening years have only to develop programs made up of these well-known managing processes: recruiting, selection, evaluation, de-

[1] See my book, *The Will to Manage* (New York: McGraw-Hill Book Company, 1966), and W. H. Newman and J. P. Logan, *Strategy, Policy, and Central Management,* 7th ed. (Cincinnati: South-Western Publishing Co., 1976).

Present Ages of Leaders of Various
Ages in Year 2000

Age at assuming leadership	Born	Age in 1977
40	1960	17
45	1955	22
50	1950	27
55	1945	32

velopment, advancement, and motivation. Of course, such leadershp programs *are* underway now in countless corporations whose present leaders care about providing future leaders: DuPont, IBM, General Electric, and General Motors come quickly to mind.

Managing Fundamentals Bearing on Leadership

In providing leaders for the year 2000, three managing fundamentals—frequently overlooked or unrecognized—should be borne in mind by the present leaders:

1. The basic ingredient of managing is decision making. Thus, managing consists of making an integrated set of decisions and directing people in executing or carrying them out.

2. Leadership is a personal skill, concerned chiefly with motivating people in carrying out decisions and in making decisions concerned with the future. But leadership itself is also decision making: determining what to do, how to act, and what to say.

3. Every decision must be made in the present—a decision must be made *now*. A plan for the future is a decision made *now*. Even a decision to decide in the future—to postpone action—is a decision made *now*.

So every person from the line operator and clerical worker to the chief executive is a decision maker, and his effectiveness can be increased by helping him make better decisions and carry them out more effectively and efficiently. To provide that help to the people at the operating level there is an organizational hierarchy of supervisors and managers, who have the authority and responsibility to make and execute decisions of increasingly greater importance as the level of authority rises. All are decision makers. All give direction to the people reporting to them.

Positions (or jobs) can be specified, duties assigned, and authority given. But the person assigned to each position brings individual personal qualities that enable him to perform the position with greater or lesser skill; and the scope and degree of his personal skills will determine his capacity to make decisions and provide direction at higher and higher levels.

It is significant that very few titles include the word "leader" and that typically leadership is not discussed extensively in business corporations, even though the very existence of the firm over time requires that leaders be produced from within or brought in from without. This is probably because leadership skills are so personal and so rare that people don't talk about them easily.

Certainly, the true leader has so much humility that he does not call himself a leader. And since leadership (unlike authority) cannot be assigned, the superior ordinarily does not like to point out to his subordinates their failure to display rare personal skills they may not have and may not be able to develop. For these subtle reasons, leadership—the greatest resource that any business can have—typically gets inadequate attention unless an organized program is sponsored by the present top leaders.

I believe that more and better programs for developing leaders are likely to be established and better results attained if a clear distinction is made between administration and management, even though most dictionaries make the terms synonymous. Administrators (or supervisors) make and execute decisions on operating matters that have been planned by managers at higher levels. Managers decide *what* shall be done, how resources shall be used. They make integrated decisions to attain balanced and optimum use of resources in achieving corporate goals. At some fairly arbitrary level, managers in most corporations are designated as "executives"; but this term is not significant for our purposes.

Administrators and managers at all levels are decision makers. All make varying proportions of day-to-day operating decisions. The more important the responsibilities of a position, the greater the proportion of decision making relating to policy, organization, and planning. And the managers at the top must make decisions relating to goals, strategy, and staffing of the important managerial positions.

All administrators and managers need the personal "people" skills for giving direction to some degree.

Thus the critical distinctions are found in the proportion of operating and policy decisions and the degrees of personal people skills required for the position. However, unless some of the senior managers develop their personal people skills to the point of leadership, the future of the enterprise is in jeopardy.

I know of two corporations where the distinction between the operating executive and the leader was recognized to great advantage. In one case an individual with leadership qualities was chosen over three outstanding operating executives who outranked him—to the surprise of everyone and to the great advantage of the corporation. In the other case the decisions of prior chief executives and boards of directors had produced only operating executives. Recently, when it came time to elect a new chief executive, the present board recognized the need for a true leader and recruited one from another corporation, which has a leadership program that produces leadership in depth. The trauma of that decision still continues as the new chief executive tries to change the company's style of managing and give personnel policies and programs real substance rather than mere form.

Distinction Between Business Leaders and Operating Managers
(Role of business leader is enclosed by dashed line)

Positions created by organization design	Personal capabilities	
	Decision-making skills	People skills
Senior managers	Goals, strategy, policy	Induce others to decide, and to execute effectively
Operating managers Administrators	Operating decisions	Direct, motivate, etc.

Consequently, the distinction between the operating executive and the leader is an important one for the board of directors to recognize and act on.

Usually, the individual progresses and grows from administrator, to manager, to leader as his interest in and capacity for leadership develop. Sometimes, the development of leadership capacity can be very rapid, and that person should be nurtured and treasured by the firm. How well the progression is monitored will determine whether a corporation develops its leaders for the year 2000.

Qualities of Leadership

The first step in the development process is to determine the qualities that leaders for the year 2000 should have. They certainly must have the fundamental qualities of leadership that remain the same over time—qualities that the leader can adapt to the role he must play and the conditions that prevail when leadership responsibility is assumed.

Much has been written on these fundamental qualities.[2] For purposes of developing *business* leadership, I believe that if the person has the qualities listed below, he is likely to have enough of the others to be a successful leader. Of course, most of these qualities apply to leadership in any field.

1. *Character.* The leader must have character and integrity that cause people to trust him.

2. *Initiative.* The leader is a self-starter. He provides the ideas and takes the risks of failure along with the chance of success. His point of view is: "Let's go—let's go together."

3. *Desire to serve people.* The leader has a belief in people. He listens to them and wants to help them grow and develop. He is a coach. This requires that he have self-confidence and humility; certainly he can't be arrogant. He is a helper, not a manipulator or a predator.

4. *Intellect.* The future business leader must have the capacity

[2] For an excellent treatment, see Robert K. Greenleaf, *The Servant as Leader.* This essay of 37 pages is available for $1.25 from the Center for Applied Studies, 17 Dunster Street, Cambridge, Mass. 02138.

to think at a high level of competence. He need not be as brilliant as many in the organization, but the complexities of business require that he be able to analyze effectively, learn quickly, and have a continuing interest in learning.

5. *Awareness and perception.* The leader not only is aware of what is going on around him—within and outside the business—but has the perception to evaluate its significance to the enterprise and to people.

6. *Foresight/Vision.* No one can successfully predict the future but the leader has the intuition, foresight, vision to sense the possibilities of what may affect the business or the people in it. He is a better guesser than others.

7. *Open-mindedness/Flexibility.* The business leader's mind is open to the consideration of new facts, new ideas. He is flexible without being flabby. He abhors the reasoning: "We have always done it that way."

8. *Persuasiveness.* The business leader is articulate (orally and in writing) and has the empathy with people that enables him to persuade rather than order them to act.

The person in a business with these qualities is just as likely to be a leader in the year 1978 as he is in the year 2000. A leader is a leader is a leader—now and in the year 2000. However, we can identify forces now at work that will probably be at work and relevant in the year 2000, when retiring leaders and boards of directors choose new leaders. These factors can serve in the meantime as guides for developing the leaders that will be needed then.

Chances are that the individual business in the year 2000 will need leaders who:

1. Are conceptual, strategic thinkers.

2. Have the capacity to cope with social forces.

3. Have an understanding of government and governmental regulation and some capacity to influence governmental forces in the interest of the public good.

4. Have the capacity to cope with internal forces in the managing of human resources.

Each of these capabilities is worth brief discussion.

Conceptual Strategic Thinking

Every leader should have capacity to think conceptually, but I believe this quality will be especially important to leaders of the business firm in the years ahead. The need is a present one, because corporate success is so much determined by external forces for change affecting the business; but these external forces will probably increase in importance in the years ahead. Thus the business leader needs the capacity to detect (awareness/perception) any type of major change—economic, political, or social—early enough to evaluate its relevance and to fashion a response to forces that are relevant to the business.

Fashioning the response calls for strategic decisions: changes in goals, objectives, and the strategy for achieving them, as well as in supporting major policies and organization structure. This requires ability to think conceptually. The conceptual thinker will almost instinctively think strategically; but if he does not, he can be trained to do so.

A "concept" is defined in some dictionaries as merely an idea. However, one or two dictionaries define it as a broad general idea drawn from specific factors. That connotation is the useful one for the business leader. Lots of people get ideas. The conceptual thinker, however, gets broad general ideas based on facts and observations—ideas that have applicability.

The following definition of the strategist by Professor Kenneth R. Andrews of Harvard Business School provides a useful guide for selecting and developing future corporate leaders:

> The strategist is concerned with combining what a company *might do,* in terms of alternatives discernible in the changing environment, what it can do in terms of resources and power, what it wants to do in terms of management values, and what it *ought to do* in recognition of the responsibility of the private firm to society.[3]

[3] From "New Developments in Corporate Strategy," speech to Harvard Business School Club of New York, May 27, 1968. This concept is developed more fully in Mr. Andrews' book, *The Concept of Corporate Strategy* (Homewood, Ill.: Dow Jones-Irwin, Inc., 1971), which every leader and future leader should find conceptually and practically worthwhile. See also *The Will to Manage,* Chapter 3, "Strategic Planning: Shaping the Destiny and Competitive Cutting Edge of the Business."

The corporate leaders of the year 2000 need to be strategists, and conceptual thinkers can be trained to think in strategic terms. The best-managed corporations today are working hard to perfect their strategic planning capability, and that effort enables them to identify and train their future leaders.[4]

Despite the conventional wisdom of the speaking platform, the rate of change is not so rapid that leaders who detect the forces cannot make the adjusting decisions as the forces unfold. For example, alertly managed corporations have had time to adjust to that most rapidly developing business tool, the computer. An article, "Fastest 25 Years" (published in IBM's *Think* magazine, January/February, 1976), traces the remarkably rapid development of the computer. Between 1946 and 1952 a series of electronic (vacuum-tube) calculators and computers emerged in rapid succession. The transistor was invented at Bell Laboratories in 1948. "But it's often a long road from invention to application. IBM and the semiconductor industry invested nearly a decade in research to . . . incorporate the solid-state technology." There was time to adjust.

The interdependent world may seem to have come about rather quickly, but it was forecast in 1943 by Wendell L. Willkie, Republican Presidential candidate, in his book *One World.* Willkie pointed out that America was "now changing completely from a young nation of domestic concerns to an adult nation of international interests and world outlook" and that "men and women all over the world are . . . beginning to know that man's welfare throughout the world is interdependent." Again, alertly managed corporations had ample time to adjust. Some made poor decisions in adjusting. Some did not detect the trend in time and made unsound acquisitions to catch up. But lack of time was not the problem—it was lack of strategic capability of their leaders.[5]

Thus it is one of the responsibilities of today's and tomorrow's top corporate leaders to detect such change factors and to lead the firm in making the correct strategic decisions.

[4] See my chapter in *The Chief Executive's Handbook* (Homewood, Ill.: Dow Jones-Irwin, 1976) entitled, "The Chief Executive as Chief Strategist."

[5] For a more complete discussion of the forces at work and problems of coping with the future, see "Gearing a Business to the Future," a section by myself and my colleague, C. Lee Walton, in *Challenge to Leadership,* A Conference Board Book (New York: The Free Press, 1975).

Coping with Social Forces[6]

A major external force that will place heavy demands on future corporate leaders is the societal demand for continuous improvement in the quality of life for the entire population. This demand is having a heavy impact on corporations now; they will be expected to participate in achieving this national goal and at the same time achieve economic success.

Richard C. Gerstenberg, former chairman of General Motors, puts it this way:

> The most successful business in the years ahead will be one that not only offers quality products at competitive prices, but also succeeds in matching its resources to society's changing demands, the business that is best able to give creative response to the social aspirations of the people it serves. Conversely the business that fails in the years ahead will be the one that fails to understand how it is related to the society around it and will, therefore, overlook opportunities for service, for growth, and for profit.[7]

Clearly, the company that is interested in developing capable leaders for the future will make it clear that those who aspire to the top levels of management must be aware of social needs and demands and be capable of directing the company's activities to meet them in a profitable way. For example, A. W. Clausen, president and chief executive officer of Bank American National Trust and Savings Association, puts it this way:

> It is imperative that the senior corporate manager understand . . . sociopolitical forces . . . in terms of their importance . . . . I would suggest this order: consumerism, demands of minorities, demands of women, and the crisis of the environment. We do not feel that anyone can aspire to a senior management position in Bank America . . . without

---

[6] For a useful and realistic treatment of this whole subject, see "Institutionalizing Corporate Social Decisions," by George A. Steiner, professor at the Graduate School of Management of the University of California, Los Angeles, *Business Horizons,* December 1975.

[7] Remarks at the Institutional Investors' Conference, General Motors Technical Center, Warren, Michigan, February 8, 1975.

an acute awareness of the impact these forces may have on our opera-tions.[8]

Thus both Gerstenberg and Clausen suggest a strategic ap-proach to social forces, with Clausen emphasizing the need for future senior managers to be aware of these forces and their impact on the business. Hence sensitivity to external forces and conceptual thinking to cope with them are further emphasized as future qualifications for top management.

In addition, however, the successful executive of the future (and the present) needs to be broad-gauged and flexible in his atti-tudes, because social forces will require changes not only in strategy but in structure, policies, and management style. The inflexible or narrow-gauged person will not qualify for future business leadership.

Governmental Relations

The trend toward increased regulation of business by govern-ment has so much current momentum that the leaders of the year 2000 will need the capacity to cope with and influence it.

The year 1976 seems to reflect some general recognition that excessive governmental regulation is so stifling to business as to be bad for the nation. But without a much greater degree of economic literacy in the electorate than we have now, our legislators are unlike-ly to exercise the independent judgments necessary to permit busi-ness firms a full opportunity to serve the public interest through maximum production of goods and services wanted by the electorate at competitive prices.[9]

So it is likely that the leaders of the future—indeed the leaders of the present—will need to be business statesmen, doing what they can to defend the private enterprise system and the market economy in the interest of the nation.

The chief executive of one of the country's largest, most progressive, and most profitable companies (a leader produced from

[8] "Standards for Top Executives," *Business and Society*, April 3, 1976.

[9] We should, of course, work to educate the electorate. The Joint Council on Economic Education (1212 Avenue of the Americas, New York City 10036), of which I am chairman, has as its purpose increasing the quantity and quality of economics taught in our schools and colleges.

within) said essentially this in a conversation with a small group: The most important thing that has happened to the chief executive in recent years is his discovery that he must deal with government so much that he can do more for his company in Washington than he can in his own office. He explained that the leader needs to understand government himself and its impact on his own company, and that he should try to help legislators and regulators recognize how the interests of the nation are best served by keeping industry productive and profitable through serving customers competitively in a market economy.[10]

Managing Human Resources

The leader of the year 2000 must be able to respond to internal forces, especially in managing human resources. These forces are now at work and can be detected, but how rapidly new ones will have impact cannot be forecast.[11] For example, in Europe representation of labor on the board of directors is required by law in some countries; and there is a trend to require that, once hired, a person must be kept on the payroll—by law in at least one European country.

More immediate forces with which to cope flow from more than a hundred individual pieces of federal legislation that directly affect the relationship between corporations and their employees. These include laws dealing with discrimination, hours of work, health and safety, equality of pay, and retirement.

At all levels there is a demand for participation in decisions affecting the individual and for jobs that are more personally fulfilling and less boring. In the article quoted earlier, Clausen of Bank America has this to say:

> The senior manager of today and tomorrow must understand in both mind and heart that new philosophical forces are changing the value systems of today's work force. The manager must see the reality behind

[10] The Brookings Institution, 1775 Massachusetts Avenue, NW, Washington, D.C. 20036, operates a number of programs to help business executives get a better understanding of the federal government and how it works.

[11] In April, 1976, The Conference Board held a major conference on "Changing Imperatives in Managing Human Resources."

job enrichment. There must be increased awareness of growing demand, particularly from younger members of the work force, for greater freedom of action, for greater responsibility, or both.

No individual will assume initiative or be fully productive in a situation in which he does not feel that his efforts contribute to shaping the ultimate outcome. He wants to feel that what he is doing is useful and important to the company, that his efforts "make a difference."

Clearly, leaders for the year 2000 must be sensitive to people and to their attitudes, feelings, and ambitions. By so doing, they will motivate employees more effectively and make their enterprise more profitable.

The Development Target (Summary)

Any business can be reasonably sure of having effective and well-prepared leaders if it focuses on finding and developing people (1) who possess the eight basic qualities discussed earlier (character; initiative; desire to serve people; intellect; awareness and perception; foresight and vision; open-mindedness and flexibility; and persuasiveness); (2) who are conceptual strategic thinkers; (3) who can lead the business in adjusting to social change; (4) who can help the business cope with governmental regulation; and (5) who can lead the business in managing its human resources effectively.

The business leader with these qualities will be a natural risk taker, because leadership inherently involves risk. The leader initiates new and innovative action; and if on average a reasonably high proportion of his decisions are not successful, he will lose his capacity to lead. Successful leadership feeds on itself while poor leadership devours itself, as the people being led make continuous evaluations of the leader's performance.

When this harsh evaluation gives the leader higher and higher marks, he develops a capacity to inspire. Thus leadership is a growth process, as the individual interacts with the situation and the people he is leading.

Business leadership typically calls for a lesser order of inspiration than leadership in other situations, such as elective office. But a capacity to inspire is the ultimate in leadership in *any* situation.

Getting Future Leaders in Place

Since the potential leaders for the year 2000 are now or soon will be on the payroll, the process for developing them should be underway now or should be started immediately. This process has two phases: (1) establishing a specific program to recruit, develop, and advance qualified individuals into leadership positions; and (2) managing the business now and in the future in a style that will attract, hold, and motivate leaders to develop.

The process has little that is new and nothing that is magic. However, suggestions can be made on each phase, based on the experience of successful companies with a record for developing leaders on a continuing basis.

Monitoring Leadership Development

Leaders must develop themselves in the setting of the business and the opportunities for leadership that it provides. But the whole process of developing on their own can be monitored in an organized manner. I believe that the concept of "monitoring" is better than the one implied in the common term: "executive development." That somehow suggests that the personnel department is responsible for developing executives and leaders. Actually, leader development must come about through the demands made on the individuals by their jobs and by the way the company is managed (management style).

But the personnel department can monitor the process so as to be sure that potential leaders are recruited; selected; identified and evaluated; given assignments that are demanding and that provide leadership opportunities; given coaching; shown examples of leadership by their superiors; given outside learning opportunities; advanced when their performance justifies it; and recognized and rewarded so as to motivate them for further development. These activities are well known and deserve only a few comments here.

1. **Recruiting.** No company can have leaders for the year 2000 unless potential leaders are put on the payroll. If the target qualities discussed earlier are kept in mind, leadership potential can be identified by skillful interviewers. Present leaders should engage in

the recruiting, and they do so in the companies most interested in developing future leaders.

A company might, in its recruiting at graduate business schools, seek to employ *only* potential leaders. The requirements to enter and graduate from these schools ensure that some of the qualities for leadership are held by graduates. A surplus of leaders need not be feared, because only a small percentage of those recruited as having leadership qualities will actually prove to have and be able to use them. Moreover, a surplus of leaders will be self-correcting because, without opportunity, some will leave for other organizations; indeed, the challenge will be to create a management style that holds enough of the best.

2. Development. Real leadership potential should be identified as early as possible and then given development assistance. Three types of development have proven themselves in practice among companies with successful records in developing leaders.

First is job rotation. Many companies give this technique lip service, but do it half-heartedly and in ways that involve little risk. The way to do it is boldly.

The second type of development that gets results is coaching. Here are some perceptive remarks from Greenleaf's essay mentioned earlier:

> *Nothing is meaningful until it is related to the hearer's own experience.* One may hear the words, one may even remember them and repeat them, as a computer does in the retrieval process. But *meaning,* a growth in experience as a result of receiving the communication, requires that the hearer supply the imaginative link from the listener's fund of experience to the abstract language symbols the speaker has used. As a leader (including teacher, coach, administrator) one must have facility in tempting the hearer into that leap of imagination that connects the verbal concept to the hearer's own experience.

Some years ago, McKinsey & Company was retained by a major corporation with a good record for developing leaders to determine what development methods had worked best. Thirty executives with the best records for developing their subordinates, as well as a number of the subordinates developed, were interviewed. Effective coaching by the superior stood out as a principal reason for development.

The third type of successful development for executives who have been identified as having real potential for leadership is outside education at one of the many programs offered by graduate business schools. These have proven to broaden the participants and open their minds more fully to developments outside the business.

3. **Evaluation.** Most well-managed businesses require written evaluations of supervisors and managers. Certainly, evaluation is important in identifying potential leaders so their development can be monitored. An effective and useful evaluation gives an assessment of performance, not of general qualities.

In many businesses, however, written evaluations have more form than substance. This will be sure to happen if the evaluators learn that their evaluations are not acted on. Conversely, when decision makers on compensation, advancement, and staffing find that the evaluations are too general or too "nice," then they give them little weight.

The answer must be found in enforcing real evaluations and then using them, beginning with the chief executive. A few companies that really care about developing managers and leaders have stimulated this and other aspects of development by not promoting executives who do not take seriously their responsibilities for developing their subordinates.

4. **Advancement.** Since individuals with leadership potential are ambitious, they expect good performance to be recognized with increased compensation and advancements to positions of greater responsibility.

I am not referring to the rapidity of advancement expected by the so-called "fast-track young tigers." Individuals in this category are typically too self-centered and too ambitious to be leaders anyway. Having little desire to serve others, they disqualify themselves as leaders, and no business should cater to them. It is better that they be allowed to satisfy their excessive ambitions in finding higher-paying jobs in other companies, as they probably will anyway.

It is important, however, that through realistic evaluations the company distinguish between the "fast-track boys" and individuals with true leadership potential—and advance the latter group as rapidly as their performance reasonably warrants. This balance is best achieved through forthright discussions with potential leaders, so they know their strengths and weaknesses and their outlook for moving into more important positions. The true leader does not expect to be catered to, but he does want recognition.

The critical relationship is that of the potential leader with his immediate superior. If the superior feels a development responsibility, he will try to motivate the potential leader to make a commitment to the company, through tangible and intangible means, recognizing that a primary function of the business leader is to bring personal goals and values in line with company goals and values.

This and all other aspects of developing leaders for the year 2000 and the years intervening can be monitored by a personnel or human resources staff. Those companies that lack such a staff—and one that is respected—had better provide one promptly.

Management Style

The way the business is managed—the style of managing—is an all-pervading, continuously operating force that determines whether the company provides future leaders (supervisors and managers as well). I have found no better definition of management style than "the way we do things around here."[12] Sometimes management style is referred to as "management philosophy."

As the term is commonly used it seems to stand for the basic beliefs that people in the business are expected to hold and be guided by—usually informal, unwritten guidelines on how people should perform. Once a management style crystallizes, it becomes a powerful force indeed. When one person tells another, "That's not the way we do things around here," the advice had better be heeded. When a superior says that to a subordinate, it had better be taken as an order. Thus management style becomes an unwritten law governing quite precisely how people shall make decisions and conduct themselves generally within the company.

Management style usually develops from practice and from following example, rather than through written guidelines for decision making and general ways of acting. Everyone down the line watches for "signals" from top-management executives on how he should manage; these signals are not what the top-management

---

[12] See *The Will to Manage*, Chapter 2.

executives *say* but what they *do.* Style also reflects the personal values of the leaders as disclosed by their actions.

Written policies and organization plans can easily be nullified by failure of top-management executives to follow them, because the unwritten law of leadership action is more powerful than the written law.

Many of the factors influencing management style are dynamic and interactive, but collectively they combine and produce a well-defined climate within the organization. This climate has a continuous and powerful influence on the attitudes and decisions and on the actions, reactions, and interactions of people at all levels. That is why management style is a continuous and powerful influence on whether individuals with leadership potential are attracted and held and whether leadership potential develops.

A management style that nurtures leaders can be planned and developed, provided the present leaders are willing to develop guidelines and then adhere closely to them in their own actions, attitudes, and decisions. A program of that sort has been mounted by the chief executive of a major corporation, who came in recently from the outside. He concluded the company needed a change in management style. So a booklet with that title was prepared, and a broad training and communications program has been set up to help executives learn the new style.

Discussion of just a few elements of style will illustrate how present leaders can manage a business so as to create a climate that develops future leaders.

1. **High ethical standards.** The individual with leadership potential will not develop—or even stay—in a business that does not meet high ethical standards. These standards must be reflected in whatever the leaders do. Moreover, a business that adheres to high principles generates greater drive and effectiveness because people know that they can do the *right* thing decisively and with confidence, with rightness being judged by adherence to ethical standards.

2. **Fact-based decision making.** A high standard for basing decisions on facts is an important feature of a management style that stimulates leadership development. Of course, every company bases its decisions on facts to a considerable degree—otherwise it would fail. However, too often decisions are based on an experience and

impaired by fixed attitudes of senior executives toward particular issues. Like so many other management concepts, however, the value of the fact-based approach depends on the degree, effectiveness, and consistency of its use. In a company where fact-based decision making is a real part of its management style, the automatic approach is "what's right," not "who's right."

The factual approach to decision making cannot be legislated. It can only be built into a company through action over time, collecting and analyzing facts and then acting on the alternative that is best in their light. Ideally, the building of the fact-based approach starts at the top. The higher the executive, the more powerful his example. But the head of any department or other organizational unit can build the fact-based approach into his unit. If he insists on facts and acts on facts, his subordinates will gladly do the same.

If the fact-based approach is a real part of management style, it will make the enterprise more flexible and hence more responsive to change, because, in the light of new facts, executives can more easily make new decisions; new facts eliminate the need for face-saving. Fact-based decision making also stimulates participative management.

Companywide respect for facts facilitates objective evaluations and lowers the barriers between levels of authority. When everyone feels that he can easily discuss facts, upward communication is stimulated and subordinates are encouraged to speak up with factual support for differences of opinion. The fact-based approach leads to fairness and better relations among people, because discussion replaces argument; and personal differences, personality conflicts, and corporate politics are minimized. Fact-based decision making also leads to better-quality decisions and improved performance generally.

3. **Freedom of action.** The individual with leadership potential—who has initiative and ambition—seeks early and growing responsibility. Management style, therefore, should encourage delegation and freedom of the individual to act on his own within the framework of strategy, structure, and policy. In fact, by making self-government of the individual a definite objective, present leaders will help produce a climate that encourages the development of new leaders.

4. **Giving work more meaning.** The people coming into the

business bring all of their individual attitudes and values developed in society generally, and they take home attitudes and values shaped by their experience at work. Interaction between conditions in the business and in society outside will help to shape their business attitudes, values, and motivations.

It should be a purpose of management style, therefore, to do whatever it can to give a high proportion of people in the business a feeling of fullfillment of some sort—e.g., that what they do makes a difference. In some way the leaders must find ways of providing personal satisfaction in the work, and this effort will stimulate development of leadership potential.

People are more likely to be motivated in their work if the leaders seek to establish compatibility of company and individual goals and encourage the individual's participation in decisions that relate to their work and working conditions. Conversely, people do not work effectively under authoritarian direction, and many companies are modifying their management style to meet this attitude. Nor does leadership flourish in an authoritarian climate.

5. Climate for productivity. Leaders do flourish in a climate that encourages productivity and where work is performance oriented.

Greater productivity can be achieved if the chief executive gives a constant demonstration of interest in productivity and communicates a sense of purpose in achieving it. For example, Texas Instruments informs all employees of company goals and actual results achieved in terms of (1) net sales per employee, (2) unit output per man-hour, (3) after-tax profits per employee, (4) assets per employee, and (5) percentage of after-tax return on assets. Communications such as these help instill a sense of productivity achievement in everyone, make productivity a real feature of management style, and help create a climate that nurtures leadership.

Many other factors, of course, determine "how we do things around here," but the foregoing are some of the principal ways in which today's leaders can create a working climate that will help to hold, attract, and develop tomorrow's leaders.

The present values in a program to develop future leaders should not be overlooked. A program for developing corporate leaders for the year 2000, and the mode of business management that it requires, will produce leaders for the intervening years as well. Moreover, a business with a management program designed to produce leaders for any period will also be well managed generally. Thus the program to develop future leaders generates important dividends and by-product benefits for the present. Underlying the program, however, must be a continuing will to manage.

MANAGERIAL QUALITIES
CALLING FOR
SPECIAL ATTENTION

"So what's new?" Implicit in much of what Marvin Bower says is that managing will not change drastically in the next twenty-five years. The primary challenge, he believes, is to find the determination—the will—to use wisely the best practices that we already have.

Nevertheless, changes will occur at least in emphasis, and some rudimentary concepts will be much elaborated. Bower examines several areas of rising significance, and our panelists placed even more weight on particular qualities that will become vital by the turn of the century. The central thrusts of these anticipated changes fall into four groups.

Agility in Coping with Change

Frequent change, often of a fundamental character, in the economic, political, social and technological environment will prevail. In Part I we noted especially the irresistible dispersion of complex, sophisticated technology coupled with marked shifts due to resource shortages. These will not be isolated events. Instead, the responses will have a ripple effect, just as the oil consumers' responses raised the threat of another OPEC boycott.

Bower picks up this theme in his discussion of strategic thinking. The future senior executive must be adept at detecting changes that significantly affect his company and at translating this new view into modifications of company strategy.

Our panelists are concerned also with the psychological aspects of frequent change. Tomorrow's managers will need confidence and enthusiasm to pursue a particular course of action while seeking ways to make that course obsolete. This sort of "planning while in motion" calls for more adaptability—and capacity to recommit oneself—than the typical graduate of our present educational system possesses.

Clearly the learning process must be a continuing one. But not all managers have the energy and skill to learn as they work. So as the pace of external and internal changes accelerates, these individuals with static ability will become outmoded. And finding one's career at a dead end can be very debilitating.

Change is not new; history testifies that we have a remarkable capacity for change. The point being stressed is that the rate and pervasiveness of future changes will strain the customary balance between enough stability to get work accomplished and enough innovation to keep in tune with the world. Future managers will have to be increasingly agile to preserve this balance.

Skill in Activating Disenchanted Employees

Motivating employees will be more difficult in the years ahead. This will arise from a shift in values and attitudes held by many, though not all, of the "new generation."

Bower notes a greater desire for personally fulfilling jobs. But what fulfills an employee is changing, as a larger proportion of employees come to work with college education. Over half the work force will have aspirations based on college exposure. Substantial frustration of these hopes is sure to occur, and we know that the behavior of a frustrated person is difficult to channel.

Other shifts in attitudes will complicate the manager's task. Skepticism about "the establishment" is an example. Badly tarnished is the belief that the corporation and government bureau act—albeit a bit slowly—with wisdom and dedication. While doubts about "the establishment" undercut commitment, a higher value is being attached to a person's own lifestyle—which often entails devoting more time and energy to off-the-job pursuits.

Of course, not all employees will be disenchanted with their jobs. Some will continue to be highly committed to company goals; some will retain the Puritan work ethic; some will feel that acceptance of a role carries an obligation to fulfill the tasks to the best of one's ability; and some will find that the work they do fulfills their personal needs. But the proportion of such people appears to be diminishing. Managers in the years ahead will have to find ways to activate large numbers of indifferent or ambivalent workers.

Unfortunately the rising importance of service industries—health, education, recreation, local government, and the like—is unlikely to relieve the disenchantment just described. While some professionals find performing such services very gratifying, more and more uncommitted workers are entering service industries. And the service establishments are becoming large and bureaucratic. The difficulties of measuring output make rewards for good performance hard to apply. So, in the service sector managers will have to devise more effective means to activate disenchanted employees.

Sensitivity to New Values

Perhaps the most elusive ability managers of tomorrow will need is sensitivity to new values—values they themselves use in making decisions.

The ground-rules keep changing. For instance, special protection for women workers, which until recently was considered a progressive practice, is now condemned as discrimination. The opening of the Western frontier has become desecration of our environment. Even more perplexing, today's new standards may be used to condemn yesterday's conduct that was quite acceptable at the time.

Ethical behavior. One set of values currently receiving much attention in the press relates to actions managers may take to further their personal ends. Just what is bribery? How can influence be used? Can divided loyalty be avoided? Under what conditions should confidential information be revealed? What sorts of discrimination with respect to employees is applauded, and what is immoral and even illegal? And so on. Local standards vary from one country to another.

It is reasonable to expect that social standards on such matters will continue to evolve. The gray areas will darken or lighten. And our future managers will be expected to perceive these changes and adjust their behavior accordingly.

Values for business decisions. More far-reaching are the values used in selecting company action. What outcomes are to be maximized, and what minimum criteria apply to other results?

The popular notion that the job of a manager is to maximize profits is a misleading oversimplification. The manager is *also* concerned with providing attractive jobs, with mobilizing materials, with harnessing new technologies, with satisfying consumer desires, with generating disposable incomes—and with a variety of other socially significant objectives.

From the viewpoint of society, the primary function of an enterprise manager is to *convert resources*—the otherwise dormant manpower, materials, technical knowledge, capital, and infrastructure—into desired goods and services. And in the conversion process he provides attractive outlets and employment for the resources. We underrate the effective manager when we say he does less.

This broader view of managing places the executive in the mainstream of many currently popular causes—such as employment of minorities (and women), conservation of material resources, and consumerism. He becomes the primary agent of reform. He is in the center of the play, not cheering on the sidelines.

Basically, however, the manager himself is not deciding which reforms are most desirable. He attempts to reconcile competing forces, adjusting first here and then there, while keeping his enterprise viable so that it can continue to serve its several publics.

Nevertheless, the manager cannot escape the difficult task of interpreting the social and legal forces whirling about him. He has the never-ending burden of perceiving, weighing, and devising a response to the diverse values thrust upon him.

The scenario for the year 2000 presented in Part I clearly pointed to marked changes in the results society expects from managers. New values will emerge that tomorrow's professional manager must find ways to absorb. The manager must be able to convert resources under changing, evolving objectives.

Integrity and self-respect. Values are merely good intentions until we actually use them to guide our behavior. The Bronfman Fellows on our panel repeatedly stressed the importance of future managers maintaining integrity by living up to their values. This, they said, is vital for both self-respect and public respect.

We have noted that both ethical behavior and values for company decisions are moving targets. These value standards surely will change over the next twenty-five years. And this evolution of standards obviously complicates the achievement of integrity.

So, although value problems for managers are not new, such problems will become more difficult and socially more important in the years immediately ahead.

Political Ability

A fourth quality that future managers will have to cultivate is political ability—or, to those who find the word "political" repulsive, diplomatic ability. Bower introduces this need when he speaks of coping with social forces and with governmental regulation, and several of the trends outlined in Part I call for a political response. By "political" we mean winning the cooperation, or at least devising an accommodation, with external groups whose support we need. Occasionally, legislation will be involved, but future managers must be active in a broader, more pervasive process.

The use of group confrontation was predicted in Part I. Consumer unions, Sierra Clubs, Women's Liberation, and OPEC are only current examples of a tide of pressure groups to come. Rarely is a purely rational, facts-on-the-table approach effective in dealing with such groups. They have an emotional commitment to a cause; their solidity depends on maintaining strong feelings; and their internal structure often lacks a mechanism for acceptance of a compromise.

Dealing with governmental agencies is somewhat similar. Although the internal structure of the agency may be set up in a familiar organizational design, the agency's existence and its continuing financial support rest heavily on political pressures. Consequently, except on routine matters, political considerations are likely to be a consideration in the agency's action—or inaction.

Business executives, nurtured in rational analysis, are often inept in the political process. Favors, power, coalitions, delaying action, face-saving, depolarization, restating issues, temporary concessions are all involved. In fact, many people are so wedded to scientific analysis that they feel politics is sordid. For the ancient Greeks, however, politics was the supreme skill—and for modern-day resolution of divergent social forces politics is essential.

With more group confrontations, rising expectations of what managers do, increasing government regulation, sharper competition for scarce resources, and social values in continuing flux, tomorrow's managers will need considerable political skill. Yet we know very little about it, and shy away from discussing it. Politics is the unexplored dimension of managing.

Summing up, then, managers in the year 2000 will need all the attributes we try so hard to develop today. In addition, several qualities will be required in greater measure. Prominent among them are agility in coping with change, skill in activating disenchanted employees, sensitivity to new values, and political ability.

PART III

SOURCES of MANAGEMENT TALENT ...
FOR THE YEAR 2000

The opportunities, the burdens, the public expectations, the social complexities facing future managers will be great. On the basis of the best forecasts available, we can predict that the need and the challenge will be unparalleled in history.

What of the prospective supply of managers to meet the challenge? Will there be enough—or too many—people adequately prepared and motivated to guide our numerous enterprises? Will they have the capacity to cope constructively with the array of changes sketched in the earlier parts of this book?

For basic enlightenment on the supply side of "Managers for the Year 2000" we turn to a set of observations by Eli Ginzberg. An imaginative and insightful scholar, Ginzberg is the world's most prolific analyst of manpower. He is the leading authority on people as an economic and social resource. His paper on sources of management talent leads to the grim conclusion that an oversupply of not very well-prepared aspiring managers will add prickly problems to those already flagged in Parts I and II.

by ELI GINZBERG[1]

SOURCES OF MANAGERIAL TALENT

All forecasts must be made tentatively and in a spirit of modesty, because the gift of prophecy has been reserved for the favorites of the gods. When an assignment involves estimating the possible shape of things a quarter century in the future, a cautious stance is necessary; even a decade is likely to produce developments beyond the ken, certainly the anticipations, of most forecasters.

To underline this point, we need only ask how many forces present on the American scene in 1970 were included in the expectations of competent analysts a decade earlier. To keep this exercise within the context of the present assignment, we will limit our examples to the manpower and managerial realms:

1. The Vietnam tragedy.
2. The burning of the ghettos.
3. Women's Liberation.
4. The rapid expansion of higher education.
5. The Great Society.

[1] I acknowledge the assistance of Anna Dutka, Research Associate, Conservation of Human Resources Project, in checking the data.

6. The longest sustained expansion of the American economy, including the leadership role of the multinational corporation.

7. The youth crisis and its challenge to authority.

The list could be expanded to include the missiles crisis and its aftermath, the passage of Medicare and Medicaid that led to the accelerated growth of the health-care industry, the revision of our immigration policy, and the many other unlikely or totally unexpected developments that did indeed occur. In the present context, the important point is that each of these developments had an impact on the demand, supply, and utilization of skilled and professional manpower.

1. THE GROWING POOL OF TALENT

Having put up a warning sign about the difficulties of intermediate and long-range manpower forecasts, we must add that such efforts are not entirely mired in uncertainty. There is a demographic foundation to manpower forecasting that provides an element of stability, especially in charting trends in managerial manpower.

To illustrate: If most managers begin their careers at about 25 and retire at about 65, it follows that, in America's bicentennial year, all persons who will be in the managerial ranks by the end of this century had been born. This eliminates one problematic element in forecasting involving people—the future trend in the birth rate. It cannot be totally ignored, however, because the availability of educated women for managerial assignments will be influenced by their decisions with respect to marriage and children.

The cohort approach provides some additional fixed points for the present exercise. It tells us that, by the year 2000, almost all individuals who are above 40 today will no longer be active.

Another observation that flows from this vantage is that the substantial majority of all who will hold managerial assignments in 2000 have not yet entered upon their careers. This emphasizes the critical importance of two formative influences: the quantity and quality of education and training that young people will receive and, equally if not more important, the range of influences to which they will be exposed once they begin to work.

Having begun with a focus on demography, we may find it helpful to stay with that approach a little longer in order to place some additional facets of the future supply of managerial manpower in context. The numbers of young people who will graduate at any future time from college or professional school is a function of the size of the age-relevant cohort, the proposition of those eligible for admission who elect to go on with their studies, and the proportion who stay the course and graduate. It should be noted, however, that the close relation that used to exist between age and attendance at institutions of higher education for degree study is being loosened; more and more students in their middle and late twenties and sizable minorities who are even older are enrolled for degrees.

As over 75 percent of the 17- to 18-year-olds are currently graduating from high school—up from about 50 percent at the beginning of World War II—the proportion of that age group who become college eligibles is not likely to increase further. But the proportion of the college eligibles who will seek to enter and the proportion who will complete their degree requirements are more problematic, since they depend on changing costs, changing value systems, and available occupational opportunities.

Since the late 1960s the proportion of white males entering college has dropped; the proportion of black males, which continued to rise for some additional years, is also down from the peak in 1972. The proportion of white women, after continuing to rise until 1971, has leveled off since then, while the proportion of black women has continued to rise.[2]

It is impossible, on the basis of a relatively few years' experience, to sort out the temporary from the more permanent factors influencing these trends. Still, it would be venturesome to assume that the college population will account for a higher proportion of the age group in the decades ahead than in the recent past.

If these two ratios—the proportion of the age group who graduate form high school and the proportion who elect to go to college—are at or close to their maximum, the size of the future college population will be determined by the numbers in the successive age cohorts. It is important to note in this connection that, by

[2] The best sources for data about enrollments in higher education are U.S. Department of Commerce, Bureau of the Census, *Current Population Reports,* Series P-20.

the early 1980s, the number of Americans reaching 18 will start to decline from a high of around 4.2 million in 1975 to a currently estimated low of 3.3 million in 1982. Once again, we must avoid straight-line projections. In the 1960s the American educational establishment ignored the incontrovertible evidence that the demand for college admission would slacken, since the number of 18-year-olds was going to level off. In the late 1970s the planners must take into account the known changes in the numbers of young people in the 1980s and 1990s.

Focus on the College-Educated Pool

We have backed into a presumption where the pool of managerial manpower has been equated with the number of college graduates. Some rationalization of this simplification should be advanced. It derives from the following: large organizations are increasingly characteristic of both the profit and nonprofit arenas in our society. One advantage that most large organizations have is their ability to offer prospective employees long-term affiliations with promotional opportunities. Since the number of these desirable jobs and careers is far fewer than the number of job seekers, large organizations are in a position to screen and pool and to select those whom they believe will be most productive. Increasingly, a college degree is a prerequisite for a managerial position.

For instance, the Armed Forces are attempting to limit their officer cadre to people with college degrees. Only college graduates are selected for pilot training, not because a college education is work-related but because the defense establishment believes that the range of qualities they seek in officer personnel is more likely to be found among college graduates—people with above-average intelligence, the ability to learn new skills, traits of character that will facilitate their socialization, and more potential for leadership. Much the same thinking undergirds the personnel selection policies of civilian organizations.

This is not the occasion to argue the logic of present-day selection procedures for managerial personnel. For our purposes we need merely note that existing selection policies are likely to be continued in the decades ahead, and if the supply of eligibles should continue to outpace the demand, it is probable that large organizations will

place an increasing importance on degrees higher than the baccalaureate.

Since college and university degrees are and will continue to be
the key criteria for the selection of managerial personnel, the following parenthetical observations are added. Potentially serious social
costs attach to a nation's supporting an education-training structure
that produces a sizable proportion of persons who will not be able to
find postitions commensurate with their training. The Carnegie
Commission has estimated that this will be the fate of more than
one-quarter of all college graduates in the 1970s. There are also
substantial hidden costs arising from the semiautomatic exclusion of
individuals without college degrees from consideration for managerial
positions. These costs are likely to weigh particularly heavily on
members of minority groups, who have greater difficulty in obtaining
the financial resources necessary to pursue an extended course of
education.

Unless the Supreme Court were to extend the doctrine of the
Griggs v. *Duke Power Company* case to the managerial ranks and
outlaw the use of all educational criteria that have not been job-
validated—an improbable development—or unless the heads of large
organizations were to institute a revolution in their personnel policies
and downgrade, even if they did not eliminate, the current heavy
weight assigned to educational qualifications, it is reasonable to treat
the college-educated pool as a first approximation to the pool of
future managerial talent.

The Academic Preparation of Managerial Personnel

We have established that the college-educated pool is a first
approximation of the source of managerial talent. Before we consider
the curricula that the university students pursue, we will address a
broader consideration. Which groups within the university–trained
pool move into managerial jobs?

1. While corporate enterprises hire a considerable number of
specialists for positions in engineering, marketing, accounting,
finance, research and development, and testing (especially
chemists), and a smaller number of graduates in more esoteric
fields such as mathematics, physics, computer sicence, and

communications, they also hire a considerable number of liberal arts graduates. Accordingly, there is no direct way of estimating what proportion of the total college and graduate pool represents the effective hiring potential. A safe conclusion would be to include all college graduates in the pool but to recognize that the probabilities of being hired differ markedly for a young person with a B.A. from a small state college with a major in physical education and for a person with an M.B.A. in finance from Harvard or Columbia.

2. Large nonprofit organizations such as hospitals, museums, social welfare agencies, and foundations are often more discipline-specific in their hiring than large corporations, because their staff and operating positions require, in addition to general skills, specific subject-matter knowledge. Moreover, they seldom are able to engage in the prolonged in-service training programs that characterize many large business concerns.

3. The fastest-growing sector of the American economy, from the viewpoint of employment, has been state and local governments. The multifarious governmental departments, agencies, bureaus, and authorities employ a large number of "middle managers," who increasingly are recruited from among the college pool. While some government hiring is directed to specialists, much of it is not restricted to persons who have completed a specific curriculum. Liberal arts graduates are able to qualify for a high proportion of all openings in government.

4. The American economy has long been characterized by considerable mobility among sectors. Concretely, a significant proportion of young people who start out in academic life and fail to obtain tenure succeed in obtaining a managerial post in a profit, nonprofit, or government organization.

5. Similarly, a considerable number of professionals, particularly individuals trained in the law, psychology, and the natural sciences, after a few years of working as a professional shift into a managerial career.

6. Again, in large organizations, particularly large business enterprises, a large number of scientists hired initially for bench work in the laboratory shift, in time, to line management.

7. Another accelerating trend is the growing proportion of well-trained persons who by necessity or choice leave their first arena of employment at the end of twenty years or so to take up a second career. This is easily seen among military personnel in their forties who, passed over for flag rank, retire from the service but almost without exception seek new employment. It may be a questionable, if not scandalous, practice whereby so many former high-ranking officers are found in the management of companies that have large procurement programs with the Pentagon, but for the present purpose reference to this mobility pattern makes the point that any comprehensive analysis must allow for shifts to second careers.

In light of the foregoing, one can distinguish three subgroups among all college and university graduates in terms of their suitability for managerial assignments. The first are those with liberal arts or education degrees, who in 1974–75 received 360,000 out of the 975,000 baccalaureate degrees awarded, or approximately 38 percent of the total. The second, and largest, contingent, which accounted for 44 percent, consist primarily of students who have majored in the physical or social sciences. They can be classified as semispecialists in terms of their preparation for management. That leaves those who have majored in accounting, business, or engineering, roughly 185,000 or 18 percent of the total, whose preparation is most directly applicable.

In developing a typology of academic preparation for management, however, there is good reason to shift the focus from the baccalaureate to the master level. To the extent that we can talk about the professional preparation for management—and surely the concept has validity—the principal focus should be on the graduates of business schools who have acquired masters' degrees in business administration or their equivalent. In the short span of a single decade—from the mid-1960s to mid-1970s—the annual output of M.B.A.s grew from about 7000 to almost 31,000, or more than fourfold. The total number of master's degrees awarded grew at a much slower rate, about one and a half times over the same period. In the mid-1970s M.B.A.s accounted for one out of every nine master's degrees awarded, and the forecast for the mid-1980s falls in the same range.

The most conspicuous change over the last decade, particularly in terms of the graduate schools of business which cater to full-time students and where the course of the program runs over four semesters, usually completed in two academic years, has been the increasing emphasis on quantitative approaches involving the techniques of operations research, mathematical model building, and econometrics. While the leading graduate schools of business differ with regard to the emphasis they place on quantitative methods, with Carnegie Mellon at one end of the spectrum and Harvard at the other, the trend has been strong and persistent and is likely to continue at least until the disciplines on which the business curriculum is based—economics, sociology, pyschology—shift their current emphases from abstractions to institutions.

As long as the present trend continues, the student body in graduate business schools will continue to be divided: those who had solid training in mathematics, at least through calculus, in their undergraduate years will have a distinct advantage over those who majored in the humanities, history, or social science.

Among the preferred graduates of the leading business schools are persons who had earlier majored in the physical sciences or in engineering, who had perhaps a master's degree along the way, and who subsequently have done well in their business courses. These broadly trained students, especially those who have also worked for several years, can usually command a premium of 10 to 20 percent in their initial salary upon their graduation from business school.

Addition of Women and Minorities to the Pool

The total of degrees awarded, as recorded above, fails to reveal the changes in the composition of the student population pursuing master's degrees with regard to either sex or race. During the last decade and particularly the last quinquennium (1970–75) there have been striking increases in the proportion of women students entering graduate business schools. At present, between one-quarter and one-third of the total student body of many of the leading schools is composed of women, and there is no reason to believe that the numbers have peaked. It should be observed that the women students are not only recent baccalaureate recipients but also include mature women who are entering or returning to the labor market and who are interested in careers. Although Harvard Business School did not admit women as regular students until 1963, once the bars were lowered the absorption of women has been free of difficulty. Most women students come well prepared; many are able to finance themselves; and although sex discrimination in employment remains pervasive, compensatory forces are operating to facilitate the placement of women graduates as a consequence of the special efforts of many large organizations to increase the proportion of women in their managerial positions.

The situation with respect to minority students is more complicated. First, they are less well prepared on the average, since many attended weak colleges. Second, the problem of financing two additional years of study is a major burden for many, even though they have access to special support from both public and private sectors. Another source of turmoil is the restiveness of many faculty members with minority students who encounter difficulty in keeping pace with the rest of the student body. Some years ago the leading business schools, responding to the challenge of the times and encouraged by foundation support, substantially increased the number and proportion of their minority-group students. Many minority students who were admitted to these schools had difficulty in meeting the prevailing standards, placing the faculty and administration in the dilemma of having to make exceptions for them or to separate them before graduation. A more satisfactory equilibrium is being established through the application of stricter standards at the time of admission. But the consequence has been a leveling of minority-student enrollments; in fact, during the mid-1970s there were reductions.

If one had to venture an estimate of future trends with respect to women and minority students in graduate business schools, a cautious position would be to anticipate rising enrollments for women until they level off in the range of one-third, and a considerably slower increase in the enrollment of black and Chicano students as a result of their lower rates of graduation from college and their difficulties in meeting the costs of two additional years of education.

But although rates of enrollment of minorities in graduate schools of business are an important index, this is by no means the sole determinant of the numbers of minority-group members who will seek a managerial career.

During the decade 1965–1975 there was a rapid increase in the numbers and proportion of young blacks attending and graduating from college. There has also been a considerable shift in the proportion attending large integrated institutions, many of which boast stronger faculty and curricula than the typical black undergraduate college. Finally, many small southern colleges have made, and are continuing to make, substantial shifts in their curricula from heavy concentration on courses preparatory for teaching to preparation for accounting, other business fields, and engineering. When allowance is made for these important transformations, the prospective increases in the number of minority-group members who will opt for managerial careers are substantial, particularly when compared to the low base of only a few years ago. To place the problem in perspective, one need only recall that the highest-ranking black man on President Eisenhower's staff with prior experience in management (Everett Morrow), was repeatedly rebuffed when he sought the assistance of the President's advisors and friends in finding a new managerial position when he left the Administration in 1960.[3]

Logistics of the Managerial Pool

Before the thrust of the preceding analysis is summarized, let us consider the relative reliance we can place on the estimates put forward. Those that rest on such demographic considerations as the numbers of young people of college age can be given greater credence than those that require selecting a ratio of that population who will attend and graduate from college. Even more problematic are the estimates that involve projections about the numbers who will seek an M.B.A. As the focus shifts from demography to economic and social forces, allowance must be made for "feedback"—that is, how considerations relating to jobs, income, careers, and lifestyles will affect the occupational choices of young and mature persons, including the strength of their interest in management.[4] The latter half of

[3] Everett F. Morrow, *Black Man in the White House* (New York: Coward-McCann, 1963).
[4] On the question of changing values, see Daniel Yankelovich, "The Meaning of Work," in Jerome Rosow, ed., *The Worker and the Job* (Englewood Cliffs, N.J.: Prentice-Hall, Inc., 1974).

this paper will address some of the more important of these institutional forces and suggest how they may impact the pool of managerial talent.

The importance of not ascribing undue weight to any statistical analysis is reinforced when we take into account qualities other than education that bear on the quality of the manager's performance, the interrelations between interpersonal and technical skills, the growing importance of franchising, and such boundary considerations as the future of legal and illegal immigration.

Immigrant Entrepreneurs

Without entering upon refinements that would require age, sex, education, and skill comparisons, we need only note that legal immigration to the United States, skewed in favor of people with scarce occupational skills, is set at 400,000 per annum, while the annual birth rate is now around 3 million. This means that, unless we change our immigration policy—and we waited 40 years before making significant changes—to neglect the flow of immigrants into the pool would be to err in our analysis. It would be an even greater mistake to ignore the number of illegal immigrants, of whom the estimates range from 4 to 14 million. There is little prospect, even if the disturbingly high rates of unemployment continue unabated, that a society that values freedom would adopt the repressive measures required to bring this illegal flow of people under control.

Although the proportion of potential managers among new immigrants is less than among the native-born, even allowing for the fact that preference for a permanent visa is given to those with scientific skills, many have considerable entrepreneurial aptitude and drive. That has surely been a lesson we have learned from recent large-scale inflows of Hungarians, Cubans, Greeks, and Chinese, and, if the past is a guide, it will also prove to be so among the Vietnamese. The American economy has interstices where foreigners who are determined to succeed can find a place to begin. While management has been viewed primarily as a planning and decision-making assignment in a large organization, money-making skills in small business enterprises cannot be ignored, since one of the dynamics of an advanced economy is in the transformation of small into larger enterprises. And it is here that the immigrant's entrepreneurial capabilities must be considered in assessing the nation's pool of managerial talent.

Self-Selection for Advanced Training

This brings us to the two additional points that bear on attempts to quantify the pool: the place of management in the occupational decision-making process of the college population and the range of skills required for a successful managerial career.

With respect to the first, the place of business within the occupational-choice matrix, two generalizations have considerable validity. The first is that a high income is an important objective in the career and life plans of large numbers of young people, and some of them appreciate that preparing for a career in business offers a path to this goal. Of course, the pervasive money-making goal can also be pursued within a great many other professions, such as medicine, law, and architecture. Therefore, the ambitious young person need not select business as his field of specialization in order to realize his pecuniary goal.

Many who choose management as a career, particularly those who attend a graduate school of business, do so by a process of elimination. They have been in the educational channel long enough to know what they do not want to do, such as pursue a doctorate in a scholarly discipline, go to law school, or become one of the horde banging for admission on the gates of the medical schools. Having considered these and other possibilities and having discarded them, they seek admission to a graduate school of business, believing that they can get a better start in their career if they enter the labor market with some additional credentials, particularly since they can look to the school's placement office for assistance in making a first connection. It would be hard to predict a rosy future for graduate schools of business if large organizations, particularly in the corporate sector, were to stop or substantially reduce recruiting their graduates. But such an eventuality does not appear on the horizon.

A closer look at the complex of characteristics associated with high performance in the managerial realm, however, points up both the strengths and limitations of a formal course of academic studies. A well-designed course of graduate studies can unquestionably deepen a student's analytical capabilities and teach him useful techniques. It may even sharpen his skills in written and oral communication. But there are three additional dimensions of critical importance for high-level performance to which the best-designed course of formal studies can contribute little. The successful manager must have a flair for the politics of organizational life—must know how to lead, with whom to enter into alliances, how to recognize and deal with opponents—all critically important skills that cannot be fully learned in the classroom. Next, he constantly needs new experiences that afford him the opportunity to broaden his knowledge and understanding of the dynamics of organizations and the complex environments in which they operate. Clearly this is not within the province of any school to provide. And finally, a critical differentiation between more and less successful managers is their capacity for sustained and directed work effort. While it would be an oversimplification to say that those for whom success at work is very important are likely to rise to the top, it is a safe assumption that in the absence of a strong work commitment a man or woman is not likely to rise above his or her peers.

More People with More Education

Aware of these additional dimensions of the complex forces that impinge on the pool of managerial talent, we can now venture a summary of our statistical and qualitative assessments, stressing once again the inherent limitations of all forecasts:

1. There is a strong likelihood that the annual pool of college graduates will continue at the current level of one million over the next decade, and that it will undergo a modest decline in the decade following.
2. The proportion of the total college group represented by women, which is now in the mid-40 percent range, is not likely to change appreciably; the proportion of minority-group members should continue to increase absolutely and relatively.
3. Because of the declining importance of education as a field for employment, it is likely that recent trends toward business preparatory courses, especially for women and minority-group students, will continue, surely for the next decade.

4. There is little if any likelihood that graduate schools of business can continue their recent rapid rate of growth, but some modest further increase in the total number of M.B.A. graduates from two-year full-time programs is likely.

5. The proportion of women among the M.B.A.'s may reach one-third of the total (conceivably even more), while the numbers and proportions of black and Chicano students will see more modest gains.

2. THE SHAPE OF THINGS TO COME

In analyzing social phenomena we must expect that all societal systems will be in constant change, often in disequilibrium. In this section we will explore some important interactions related to changes in the managerial pool.

Continuing Education

We begin with the cumulative effects of the expanding managerial pool, the result of the enlarged influx of trained persons. Between the mid-1960s and the mid-1970s the number of baccalaureates awarded annually almost doubled and the number of M.B.A.'s increased fourfold. The higher numbers of degrees awarded are likely to be maintained in the decade ahead, and there might be a still further, if modest, increase in the annual output of M.B.A.'s.

The question that immediately confronts an economist is: how long will it be before such an enlarged supply will impact on the demand for and utilization of managerial manpower? We should recall here the point made earlier of an adjustment process that was at work in the 1960s and again in the 1970s: some positions previously filled by high school graduates are now reserved for college graduates. Not much is known about the correlates of this upward drift in job requirements, which is determined less by changes in technology and more by the increased availability of better-trained people. Scattered evidence suggests that the earnings of the college trained are beginning to weaken relative to those of the less educated. But there is growing, if still limited, evidence of an increasing restiveness among many college and university graduates in middle management positions as the result of their unmet expectations related to the underutilization of their skills. Logic would point to this, since executives with significant decision-making power in a large corporation may not exceed a hundred—that is the number that General Motors identified in a recent annual report.

The prospective imbalance between requirements and availability of managerial personnel is more complicated. Some years ago Harold Smiddy, one of the principal architects of the post-World War II reorganization of the General Electric Company, advanced the proposition that the rapidly changing knowledge-techniques and sociopolitical environments in which business operates underscored the desirability of requiring all managers in their early forties who are scheduled to advance to the higher rungs of their organization to return to school for eighteen months or so to refurbish their intellectual capital. This points to the continuing obsolescence that must be taken into account in analyzing the managerial pool.

Two matters are related to both the underutilization and the obsolescence of middle management skills. The first points to the relatively small social, organization, and personnel costs involved in a much enlarged system of continuing education. If it is true, as I believe, that most organizations tend to accumulate too many people in their middle management ranks, with the result that many encounter difficulties in making full use of their time and energies, then the broadened opportunity for middle managers to pursue in-house and external educational opportunities might prove a constructive and satisfying balance-wheel. If such an approach to solving the problem of excess time is not to create another—rising expectations that cannot be met, at least within the same organization—the purpose of additional education would have to be more closely related to goals of self-development and less to career advancement. The second points to the fact that better-educated, more knowledgeable, and more alert individuals would be better positioned to advance, especially in an economy in which there is likely to be more intersectoral mobility and where fewer and fewer individuals will be interested in spending their entire lives within a single organization.

If the foregoing prognostication turns out to be a fair one, we will have to anticipate a substantial increase in the number of individuals who will pursue an M.B.A. during the years when they are actively engaged in earning a livelihood. Since the University of

Chicago's School of Business has an enviable record of catering to an employed group, and since other graduate schools of business, including Columbia's, are moving to introduce or expand similar types of programs, we can expect rapid growth of continuing education courses.

Women Managers

It will take the better part of another decade before a significant number of women move into the higher ranks of management, but it is not too early to outline some of the consequences of such a development. The experience of the military and selected experience in the civilian economy, particularly in the foreign service and academic life, have led personnel managers to modify existing policies and procedures pertaining to married couples in the same organization. For instance, the only prospect of retaining couples within an organization that requires its personnel to go overseas on terms of service of three to four years is an assignment system that enables both of them to be located on the same or an adjacent post.

A second adjustment is the need to remove conventional barriers against hiring spouses. While there may be reasons of propriety and equity to avoid hiring one spouse who will report to the other, the more wide-reaching regulations proscribing nepotism are increasingly anachronistic, particularly because of new laws and regulations relating to equal opportunity.

Since many large organizations will probably continue to balk at hiring both spouses for managerial assignments, it is likely that there will be a broadening of the informal reciprocal arrangements that now exist with regard to the hiring of the sons of senior executives. Large organizations accommodate each other in the placement of these young people to prevent their having to work for the organization in which their fathers have major roles.

Another likely consequence of the increasing number of couples pursuing dual managerial careers is increased difficulty for management in reassigning junior, middle, and top managers. Europeans have long remarked on the frequent relocations that are characteristic of the personnel practices of many American corporations. It is not unusual for a junior executive on his way up to have to relocate five times in ten years. It has been assumed that his wife and children had no special claims to consideration, for, after all, the man was moving up in pay, status, perquisites. What more could his family want?

When more and more married women begin to have careers of their own with pay, status, and perquisites approaching those of their husbands, corporations will not be able to assume that their managerial personnel will be so mobile. A substantial salary increase and advancement in rank for one of the spouses will scarcely compensate for the losses sustained by the other if he or she must resign from a $30,000-a-year position.

Many other changes are likely to occur when women move increasingly into the higher ranks of management. Professor William Goode has sketched some of the more subtle changes in relationships and institutions that are the likely outcome of this revolution.[5]

Toward Equal Opportunity

About a decade ago, one of America's leading manufacturing companies promised an attractive black student about to graduate from the Graduate School of Business at Columbia University a position in its marketing division with the clear understanding that his territory would not be delimited to black clinetele. The company reneged on its promise and at the end of a year the young man found a new position. This episode helps to date the special treatment of minority-group managers.

Another story is relevant: a decade or so ago a major chemical company was pressed to explain why it had so few minority personnel on its staff. The reason lay not with discriminatory hiring or promotion policies, the company said, but with the inability of black persons to find suitable housing in the southern communities where many of the company's plants were located.

Racist policies and practices that infuse the entire social system will not yield to a simple head-on attack on employment. Discrimination in housing, in club memberships, and in informal social relations are intertwined with broadening opportunities for

---

[5] On the female manager, see William Goode, "Family Life of the Successful Woman," in Eli Ginzberg and Alice M. Yohalem, eds., *Corporate Lib: Women's Challenge to Management* (Baltimore and London: Johns Hopkins University Press, 1973).

minority-group members to rise in the managerial hierarchy. Many of the key relationships on which a person's future in the organization depends reflect the ties that he or she makes in hours off the job—at dinner, on the golf course, on vacation. Accordingly, we must anticipate that even with the hiring bars lowered and eventually removed, most blacks and other minority-group junior executives will encounter continuing difficulties in climbing up the organizational ladder by virtue of their substantial social isolation from their peers and superiors.

Note should be taken also of increasing competition not only between white and minority-group males but between both men and women in all groups for the relatively small number of good jobs that exist in every organization. To paraphrase the comment of the late chief psychologist of duPont, there is little room at the top.

Authority versus Professionalism

Large organizations derive much of their strength from being structured so that basic responsibility for determining policy resides at the top, while those in the middle and lower management understand what is expected of them and are willing to follow the policies and routines determined at the top.

But professionals view the manner in which they work—and often the goals toward which they work—as partially or wholly within the orbit of their own determination. Accordingly, the steady efforts to professionalize management carry with them an implicit challenge to preexisting structures of authority and legitimacy. If an individual is well educated, if he has been encouraged to weigh alternative goals and the paths of reaching them, his resistance to carrying out uncritically orders from above will be substantial.

It would be risky to estimate the rate at which the challenge to authority is growing, but there is little risk in suggesting that, during the next quarter century, the steady loosening of the hierarchical structure of large organizations must be anticipated, even if the consequences and adaptations thereto remain unclear.

The effects of the challenge by professionalism to those with formal authority can be found in the spate of troubles characterizing many of our society's major institutions, whose leadership has come under increasingly severe attack—in the arenas of religious, military, governmental, corporate, and academic life.

The Changing Contours of Education, Work,
and Leisure

If our earlier emphasis on continuing education is considered along with the underutilization of the skills of middle management and the growing thrust of professionalization, and if account is taken of the broader trends in the economy, we may expect the United States as well as other developed nations to enter an era when the long-established patterns of preparation, work, and leisure will undergo substantial transformations. The separation of these several functions within the life cycle has begun to give way at the edges; managers spend more and more time in continuing education, professors take more sabbaticals, work schedules are adjusted prior to retirement, individuals undertake consulting and other employment ties after retirement, there is increasing flexibility about the age of retirement, options are broadened with respect to types of fringe benefits that managers may select—all of these arrangements point to even larger changes in the role of work in the decades ahead.

Unless the developed economies enter upon a period of no or much reduced growth, which I see no reason to anticipate, it is more or less certain that, with the family income of the managerial group continuing to rise substantially, and with most families having fewer children, men and women will seek to alter the long-established patterns of being short of time in their active years and long on time after their retirement. It is hard to believe that the existing pattern yields optimal satisfactions for most successful men and women. Accordingly, we must anticipate that pressures will mount, conceivably quite rapidly, for experimentation that looks to lessened rigidities and greater options.[6]

Concluding Note

As this piece concludes, it is well to repeat the warning with which it began. The future is revealed only to prophets. The rest of us must be satisfied with making rough estimates about what in the

[6] For additional perspectives on some of these themes, see Eli Ginzberg, *The Manpower Connection: Education and Work* (Cambridge: Harvard University Press, 1975), and *The Human Economy* (New York: McGraw-Hill, 1976). See also Margaret S. Gordon, ed., *Higher Education and the Labor Market,* Carnegie Commission on Higher Education (New York: McGraw-Hill, 1973).

existing social structure appears to be stable and what is undergoing change. If the changes are potent, they will affect the more stable sectors, which in turn will manifest accelerated transformations.

This analysis has focused on the changing pool of managerial talent. Among the more interesting trends we are able to identify were broadened participation by women and minorities, increasing professionalization, and the threat of substantial underutilization. The analysis called attention to a few of the likely changes that these developments would bring about in managers' life styles, the organizations for which they work, and the larger society by the year 2000. But the nature of these changes cannot be specified; we have merely sought to identify some of the mechanisms that will determine them.

RESPONSES TO OVERSUPPLY

The fourfold increase in the flow of M.B.A.s will surely swamp the demand. As Ginzberg notes, to the traditional white male supply of potential executives we must add both women and minority candidates. With expansion from these sources, enrollments in managerially oriented business courses will probably continue at peak levels. But the need for new managers, especially at the senior levels, is growing at a much slower pace. The inevitable outcome will be very sharp competition for managerial jobs.

A vital qualification must be added. This large supply of potential managers will not all possess the skills, attitudes, and knowledge required. While formal management education of young people is indeed helpful, native ability and qualities drawn from experience are also necessary. In fact, one study indicates that many in the large influx into business schools are weak in "motivation to manage."[7] Moreover, the business schools may not be preparing their students to meet the new managerial challenges sketched in Parts I and II. So a college degree does not always signify a person is qualified to become a manager.

Nevertheless, student expectations are high. These aspirations for high managerial posts are based on several factors: past successes

[7] J. B. Miner, *The Human Constraint: The Coming Shortage of Management Talent* (Washington, D.C.: Bureau of National Affairs, Inc., 1974).

of M.B.A.s, the emphasis and presumptions in business courses, active recruiting by large firms, and only mild weeding-out of the less gifted students from kindergarten to graduate degree. As a result, thousands of young people each year are reinforcing their anticipations of becoming, if not a president, at least a high-level manager.

The stark reality is that many of these expectations cannot be met. There simply will not be enough room at the top for all the contenders. Ironically, while we have more expectant candidates than places, we may also face a shortage of people with the particular blend of qualifications that the prevailing situation demands. Our best forecasts indicate that the logistics of managerial supply are in disarray.

The focus of comments by symposium panelists, then, did not challenge Ginzberg's estimate of supply. Instead, the central concerns were the likely responses to the oversupply as it develops. Important among the possibilities are the following.

1. Part of the oversupply will become *disillusioned and withdraw* from the race. A few will withdraw entirely—find a deserted New England farm or a relative's summer home and pursue a hobby. More of this group will hang on cynically but do little to rectify their own situations. The spectre we must try to avoid is a large cadre of "overeducated misfits"—such as exist in India and the Philippines— who can't find jobs matching their expectations but, because they possess a diploma, are unwilling to take positions below their dignity. With American traditions and mobility, a more likely response is to try another career. Even with these drop-outs subtracted, the supply of expectant managers will be large relative to the demand.

2. The keen competition for good managerial jobs will heighten the pressure for *legalistic* resolution. "Equal rights" based on age, sex, color, religion, deportment, residence, ancestors, school tie, and the like will be demanded; formal, legal procedures probably will become more common. On the other hand, socially acceptable bases for discrimination will be promoted. Various certifications and professional examinations will be proposed to identify and protect the elite.

Legal measures may improve the equity in selection, but in the foreseeable future they will not significantly reduce the total supply of candidates. Only the basis of competition will change. There is, however, serious danger that widespread pursuit of the legal approach will so complicate managerial selection that adequate but not the best candidates will win appointment.

3. Quite aside from such legal means intended to ensure individuals of open competition, both companies and aspiring managers will seek *constructive differentiation.* Skills and knowledge that distinguish a person from the pack will be significant. These will be capabilities directly relevant to company needs. Just as in a market for products, when the supply becomes ample the imaginative suppliers try to differentiate their wares in ways that better serve the users.

4. Even *more education* is in prospect—especially continuing education for managers already in jobs. Such education will aid in the constructive differentiation and in the certification projected above. Also, changing managerial requirements will call for "retooling." With a continuing inflow of aspiring managers those already on jobs will have to keep abreast of new knowledge and advanced skills.

5. The predicted sharp competition for managerial positions will create pressure back on educational institutions for *"useful," relevant, productive education.* The universities, caught up in their own bureaucratic web of degree-granting to young people, may be unable or unwilling to adapt their activities to serve more mature students. If they don't adapt, other organizations will fill the need. Evidence is already at hand that professional associations, trade associations, consultants, and large companies are ready to step into this growing market (continuing education can be self-supporting).

Our analysis of the supply of management talent has dealt almost entirely with the flow of aspiring managers through formal management education. We do not mean to imply that formal education has a monopoly. Managers will continue to rise from diverse sources, and companies will play the key role in the development of persons from the time they become first-line supervisors. We have focused on formal education because increasingly in the United States that will be the major source of managers; it will also be at the center of oversupply, and it has high potential for contributing to qualitative changes.

PART IV

WHO SHOULD DO WHAT...
TO PREPARE FOR THE YEAR 2000?

Prediction is not planning. Prediction is passive; it merely seeks to foretell what is likely to occur. In contrast, planning implies an intent to shape future events, at least to the extent of deliberately adjusting to predicted forces. Planning can be constructive; it presumes that we can, if we try, make the world a wee bit better place to live.

The first three parts of this book are concerned with prediction. First we looked at a sample of the major pressures that will alter our environment—exploding population, a scramble for energy, steps by third-world countries to improve their lot, the new biology, an aging educated work force, shifts in values, group confrontations, and the like.

Next we considered ways in which such a changing environment might alter managerial skills that will be in high demand. Here we predicted a change more in degree than in kind; greater agility in adjusting to changes, political skill in dealing with group confrontation, competence in motivating "turned-off" employees, and, by no means least, more responsiveness and integrity in dealing with value issues. And at the same time that the management job becomes tougher, society's standards for managerial performance will become more exacting.

In Part III we considered the supply of managers to meet this challenge. The outlook on this side of the equation is for an over-supply of aspiring managers—leading to disillusions, resort to legal tactics to secure jobs, and efforts to achieve differentiation on the basis of professionalization and certification. But despite this scramble for good jobs—or perhaps because of it—we find no clear assurance that the leadership qualities of available talent will be matched to the tasks that lie ahead. In fact, if we continue on our present course, we will have too many people with unrealistically high expectations and too few with the will and the skills most needed.

Part IV turns from predictions to the question of who should do what to prepare for the year 2000. Opinions differ. Some think we should sharply modify our educational process. Others believe companies should alter their organizational structure. A few are so bewildered by future uncertainties that they retreat to a wait-and-see refuge.

Because of this diversity of proposals, our symposium considered ideas of several experts. We sought innovative ideas, areas having high leverage, directions where improvement is likely to yield to large payoffs. The authors of papers were asked to focus briefly on one or two points they felt could be especially helpful.

The papers and the ideas emerging from our discussions take three viewpoints. First is a fresh review of what is happening in Europe. Second, proposals for U.S. education are highlighted. And third, ideas for companies and individuals on the job are summarized.

A. NEW EUROPEAN DRIVE FOR MANAGERS

One unexpected outgrowth of the U.S. company invasion of Europe in the 1960s is a vigorous effort by European countries to improve the quality of their own managers. Few Americans realize that much more innovation in management development is taking place in Europe than at home. Anthony C. Hubert, who is Secretary General of the European Association of National Productivity Centres, has an excellent vantage point upon these thrusts. Although each country has its own social structure and traditions, the various efforts Hubert describes in the following paper are at least suggestive of directions we might pursue.

by **ANTHONY C. HUBERT**

A NEW GENERATION OF EUROPEAN MANAGERS

This paper considers the magnitude, recent origin, momentum, level of managers, kinds of subjects stressed, and leading sources of finance for the greatly expanded management development activity in Europe.

Future Pressures on European Management

Quantitatively, various estimates[1] concur that people in managerial functions constitute about 2 percent of the total population. Hence, western Europe has some six million managers, and this number is likely to rise to some nine million if the movement toward a "postindustrial society" continues. Even in Federal Germany and Sweden, where the movement toward a postindustrial society is not taking place, managers will increase in numbers. For in its internal structure manufacturing is moving toward more knowledge-intensive industries, which have a greater proportion of managers than the traditional manufacturing firms.

Qualitatively, a number of strong currents will increasingly affect enterprises, their managers, and hence "management" and

[1] Gaston Duerinck, "Le Point de Vue European," in *La Formazione dei Quadri come Investimento* Italy: ASFOR, 1975.

"business" schools.[2] Foremost here are the changing values within European society; many accepted corporate practices of a decade or two ago have been subjected to vociferous criticism and waves of legislation. Of particular significance, economic aims take undisputed precedence over social aims; if the market economy system was generally accepted when its economic results were good, it no longer is when its economic performance declines (although it is difficult to see what can effectively or efficiently replace it). Furthermore, there is a growing feeling that nonmanagerial groups not only *can* but also *should have the right to* erode the enterprise system's considerable power. The power in question is both economic (the creation of wealth, the determination of employment, the influence over big government) and social (its influence on such key institutions as the family and the educational system).

The *repercussions* of this value shift concern both the physical operations of the enterprise, such as working conditions and environmental pollution, and its overall direction and day-to-day management. Changes are occurring in the following directions:

1. More people have the right to detailed information about the real economics of the company.

2. More aspects of company activity are being subjected to negotiations.

3. Thus, more people, both inside the company and out, are able to affect decisions in the company in various ways.

4. There will be more opportunity for criticizing management after it has acted.

5. The people who will acquire greater influence over the company are those who now have no responsibility toward it.[3]

These thrusts mean that there will be, first, an increasing

[2] In Europe a "management school" or "business school" is a paraprofessional institution deriving its finance from both enterprises (private and public) and the state; such schools serve the management community but remain rather independent of it, and in general they are only rather loosely connected with a university. These schools generally do not operate at the undergraduate level.

[3] Par Torner, *A propos Management* (Swedish Employers' Confederation, 1975).

demand to stop training individuals simply in managerial skills and techniques ("training mercenaries for the highest bidder"[4]) and, second, a greatly increased need to encourage more *entrepreneurship.* Both require moving away from the administratively efficient but somewhat lethargic structures that have characterized "well-managed" organizations. Thus, management schools will have to "foster the kinds of behaviors and attitudes that result in more openness, in more teamwork, in greater orientation toward the future and toward the consumer, and that develop an orientation toward performance and an acceptance of individual responsibility."[5] Let us look at significant trends in this direction.

Responses from Education

The first aspect is the sheer size. European countries have been making considerable efforts to increase the throughputs of business and management students at undergraduate, graduate, and postexperience levels, but since the base was very small, the outcome has remained elitist. From smaller beginnings in Belgium, the United Kingdom led the way with a central foundation (collecting money from companies) and two major business schools. But it was probably in France that the most massive and significant effort was made. Launched in the late 1960s and stimulated by the "événements" of May 1968 (a very concrete manifestation of "changing values"), this program sent several hundred French management teachers for master's level training in North America. This corps of new professors has greatly increased the output of the French university and allied system (chambers of commerce support a national network of university-level schools of management), and in doing so it has changed the quality of the "product" in a way symptomatic of the situation elsewhere in Europe. Trained in techniques and skills, the faculty developed critical—but not necessarily negative—attitudes and behaviors toward business.

This *critical attitude,* transmitted to the students, is working for internal change in the larger organizations, but not necessarily

[4] Gaston Duerinck, quoted in *International Management Development,* Vol. 3, 1975, EFMD, Brussels.
[5] Dean Berry, "Continuing Education in Management in Europe: A Danger at the Crossroads," mimeographed (INSEAD), 1975.

elsewhere. Europe in the future will have to pay much more attention to bringing basic concepts of sound management to the *masses.* The top quartile of companies may have been fairly well served, but the mass of the smaller companies has not been reached. This will require insertion into post-primary educational systems not only of basic managerial concepts (and indeed of those of technology) but also of the feel for working life. Only massive recourse to educational technology (as already evidenced in Belgium and Holland, for instance) can possibly dent the problem.

However, the activity in France does not mean that all European countries will increase the output of their management or business courses at *undergraduate level.* In West Germany, for instance, a large proportion of future managers are trained in the traditional business economics area, which is becoming more mathematical but no more behavioral—and the experiments with new approaches begun in the mid-1960s have come to little. Elsewhere, although the concepts of multidisciplinity and "polyvalence" have won further acceptance, "management studies" are by no means accepted as conferring the understanding and skills required of the future manager and entrepreneur. "In their recruitment and selection employers attach more much importance to general qualities— aptitude, initiative, social skills, confidence, and wide interests—than to degree subject."[6] This attitude does not necessarily reflect on amateurism in business management. For one thing, the mosaic variety in European culture is felt to call for diversification of background in and between countries, albeit interwoven with some basic concepts. For another, past failures in specialized approaches—for instance, the eastern European emphasis on cybernetics in the 1960s—if multiplied on a massive scale could well have occasioned massive crash reeducation programs, if not disaster.

So the *role of the university system* in the training of future managers has hence undergone little basic change; it is to train the critical mind, to filter out the best brains, with the management schools training an increasing percentage of this selected population to "jump through further hoops."[7]

[6] PEP Broadsheet No. 557, Sandwich Courses in Higher Education, PEP on CNAA Degrees in Business Studies, 1975.
[7] Lumsden, K., "Pedagogical Innovation," paper delivered at Conference of the European Foundation for Management Development (EFMD) on *Innovations in Management Education,* Brussels, January 1976 (mimeograph).

A common element in effective approaches serving the more immediate requirements of business is that of *action learning*. Here the mass approach is adapted to individuals, characteristics, and learning focuses on and is directly connected with real problems. The central aim is to ensure the greatest possible coincidence and reinforcement between stints in educational settings and learning in the work organization. Meaningful learning is encouraged and irrelevant learning avoided by the focus on real company problems.[8] Such approaches are already infiltrating the university system, causing faculty members to do less teaching of what they themselves know and to more work as "awareness agents" and "resource people."

Striving for relevance has brought about two further trends. The first is that large organizations, public and private manufacturing and services, have devoted massive resources to *internal management education*. At the outset mainly technical, these programs have developed through the phase of "developing the organizational spirit" to that of understanding the meaning of environmental changes—particularly in values—for the organization.

A trend that is just emerging is for *management schools* to become more intimately *embroiled with* training with *individual companies*. This has led to the creation of whole new schools as well as to significant transformation elsewhere; already some of the largest schools catering mainly to the postexperience manager devote about one-third of their man-hours to (and generate somewhat more of their annual budgets from) such activities. This very proximity is not without problems; schools can be pressured to undertake activities more for their own financial gain than for the betterment of the subject organization, and they run the risk of perpetuating current practice to the detriment of research. But the schools heavily involved in this field are developing some of the most significant research work in Europe.

Broad acceptance of this concept and that of "recurrent education" is making considerable amounts of *money* available for adult education, particularly that of a vocational nature. Perhaps because of its importance (or because of the dexterity of the management educators) management education has benefited more than commensurately; of the 1 percent of payroll required by French law to be

[8] Ashmawy, S. & R.W. Revans, *The Nile Project: An Experiment in Educational Autotherapy.* Southport, U.K.: ALP International Publications, 1971.

devoted to recurrent education by companies there [representing, in 1975, some $2.5 billion (U.S.)], 10 percent was spent on managers. This represented a training stint sometime during the year for more than one corporate manager in three, compared with one working man in seven (facts that contain the germs of future political discord).

Less well known is a similar type of training levy in Norway, which is split three ways: somewhat more than half goes to the trade unions for their training programs, somewhat less to the employers' bodies, and the remaining 5 percent to the joint "cooperation council." Much of this money is used to develop the ability of members of the traditional *adversary parties to cooperate* for the betterment of the firm and the collectivity, within a rapidly evolving and innovative corporate structure. Though training is undertaken separately for workers and shareholders/owners/managers, there is a tendency for more joint training efforts to be carried out within companies. Socially determined, such approaches can have major beneficial economic consequences, for not only do they enhance "industrial peace" (which some Scandinavians consider their major business asset) they also release many entrepreneurial ideas from the work force.

The forced availability of money has enticed entrepreneurs to develop *new instruments.* Swedes have blazed the trail with a series of publications, "Look After Your Firm," which are being adapted and translated into all the major European languages. Such do-it-yourself kits can be used by all types of organizations, private and public, for a variety of purposes. Though experience shows that they require back-up services by specialists, they seem to have an ensured future, especially for "mass approaches."

Management education cannot remain national if management is becoming increasingly *international.* A first series of reactions here has been to run courses on international management and to create and develop international schools. But the international school is a rather costly body that can touch only a very small amount of the "market." Rather, there will have to be a growing number of bilateral and trilateral relationships between schools. Significantly, the first cooperative approach in Europe has been between the more vocationally oriented schools. But national cooperation is also required; the three universities of the Scottish Business School have pooled their efforts to develop its international management program, and the Canadian government has recently helped launch four centers across the country specializing in different aspects of international business. Not only short- but also long-term faculty exchanges will become more numerous, particularly as new national structures are set up to accommodate them (for instance, the new Swedish institute for multinational enterprise) and as Anglo-American becomes the common language of communication among the non-English.

ENERGETIC SEARCH FOR EFFECTIVE MANAGEMENT DEVELOPMENT

Hubert reports a twentieth-century Reformation in management development. In Europe both new institutions and new techniques are being vigorously created. These vary from country to country, and include:

1. New major business schools.
2. "Action learning."
3. Management education within companies.
4. Management schools that provide in-company training.
5. Specific tax support for company educational activities.
6. Training in management-labor cooperation.
7. Do-it-yourself kits for small firms.
8. International faculty exchanges.

Permeating all these efforts is an increased stress on social values. Also evident is an objective, critical attitude toward current business practices.

The European universities have not been pioneers in this movement. With a few exceptions, they have lacked the necessary flexibility and a willingness to be relevant. So typically the initiative has come from outside, with subsequent, loose university affiliation sometimes being arranged. Nevertheless, it is a movement of a very substantial magnitude and potential impact.

For years the United States had a great technological lead in management concepts and managerial development. And we smugly exported that technology. Now we have little reason to presume that this international trade will remain unbalanced.

B. NEW DIRECTIONS FOR BUSINESS EDUCATION

The short-run market test of business education in the United States is favorable. Enrollment is good; the products are salable; income is adequate to assuage avaricious university controllers. But if predictions sketched in Parts I, II, and III are accurate, business educators dare not rest on their current economic laurels. Today's products will have qualitative disadvantages in tomorrow's market; and the supply/demand balance will force much more product differentiation. (There are even doubting Thomases who say today's product is not all that it should be.)

So, a whole cluster of suggestions on "who should do what" are directed at formal business education. Two of our short papers have this focus. One by Robert K. Greenleaf proposes a sharp departure from the prevailing pattern of education. Greenleaf is a prophet from within the business establishment. He has had a long and distinguished career in American Telephone and Telegraph Company, where he promoted many of the Bell System's pioneering efforts in executive development. He is widely regarded as one of the most profound thinkers about managing business enterprises. If his proposal is jarring, remember that it comes from a very well-informed person not inclined to make rash statements.

by **ROBERT K. GREENLEAF**

CREATIVE, REALISTIC LEADERS

The only things I am sure about regarding the year 2000 are that it will be different and that I cannot foresee the details of what it will be. Neither could I have foreseen the present circumstances when I entered business just 50 years ago.

The managers of today, it seems to me, are able to cope with current conditions as well as did those who were in charge when I joined them in 1926. And the situation today is as different from 1926 as the year 2000 is likely to differ from the present. We have made it up to now; and we will continue to make it—if we make it—because a sufficient number of able people are adaptable and creative and they tend to assert leadership and grow with their experience.

It could be that we will face conditions in the year 2000 with which humans, as they are then prepared, cannot cope. But I do not believe it is feasible to try to anticipate those conditions in detail in the hope that we can prepare young people for some speculative situation that does not now exist. The risk is too great that we will prepare them for the wrong things, and thus add confusion to what is likely to be an exacting task. Besides, I believe there is an instinctive wisdom built into most of us that will resist the effort and render it futile. We need to look ahead, but not that far ahead. It is more important to prepare the young to cope with conditions immediately

confronting them and set them firmly on a course of adapting creatively, asserting leadership, and growing with their opportunities.

The view of the future today is different from what it was
fifty years ago, I believe, because we are much clearer that there will
be change, and we have a new awareness that the social order is in a
precarious state—and we know that we can do much better to assure
the future.

How can we do better? (1) Launch a new effort to prepare
young people for the future, an effort that is reasonable and possible
with available resources—human and material—an effort that will
have the effect of better using what we now know to help them build
an adaptive creative stance toward their environment, to assert leadership, and to grow with their experience as long as they are alive. (2)
Stop doing things that we are now doing in a big way that block such
development. *Who should do what about these matters?* This is the
question that has been addressed to me.

I am reasonably sure of my ground concerning only what
might be done in the fourteen-year span from ages 14 to 28. Surely,
there is much to be done before 14 and after 28, but I have no set-
tled views about those periods. I suggest the following steps, not as
final or absolute solutions, but simply to help define areas where
concentrated thinking is needed—about things to do, and things to
stop doing.

1. We need a new concept of education, and the place to start,
I believe, is with colleges and universities. This is not necessarily
where attention is most needed; but, because colleges and universities
have some autonomy as separate institutions, and because so many
of them are largely privately funded and are being pressed financially,
they may be more open to innovation.

I cannot find a good rationalization to justify expanding academic collegiate education from the 15 percent of the college-age
population that was served prior to World War II to about 50 percent
now. The GI subsidies at the close of the war, one of the most sen-
sible steps we ever took as a nation, gave higher education a powerful
growth stimulus, and we seem just to have kept on going without
much thought as to whether this was a good idea. And we did it in
the face of informed opinion that such education was not right for
more than about 15 percent of the population. I recall John Gardner's
pungent title to his editorial in his last report as President of the Car-

negie Corporation ten years ago. He referred to *The Antileadership Vaccine* that our whole society, led by the colleges and universities, was administering to the young. In the past ten years I have had a good deal to do with colleges and universities and I agree with John Gardner, they are administering an antileadership vaccine—and quite effectively.

They need to stop doing that and administer a proleadership vaccine!

And who will see that they do it? In my considered judgment, the trustees of these institutions will assert their proper role and see that it is done. The nature of university governance is such that this step is not likely to be taken without some sustained and informed urging from trustees (and trustees will need some help—from other than faculty and administrators).

If the trustees will not give this leadership, then I fear that the position that Governor Brown of California is reported to have taken may prevail: "I intend to starve the university system into reform." I hope it does not have to come this way because, as we well know from the tragedies of the late 1960s, the universities are fragile institutions and there is much that is precious that may be lost if they are dealt with harshly.

If we produce leaders and managers who can deal creatively with the conditions of the year 2000, even if those conditions are no more exacting than those we face today, then the universities, in addition to all of the other valuable things they now do, will become the affirmative nurturers of qualities of adaptability, creativity, and the disposition to assert leadership and grow with experience. The universities ought to do at least as well by potential leaders as they do with athletes—and the two opportunities have this in common: neither is basically academic, although there is much to be learned.

2. Those who stand outside the universities and who have some resources at their command (individuals, businesses, foundations, governments) can take one prudent initiative to lead universities toward this objective with little risk of harm. They can earmark part of their giving to support a new extracurricular offering, not for credit and under the immediate direction of the president of the university, for a special program for those students who can be identified on entry as having high potential for carrying responsible (for the public good) leadership roles in the future. Many such students

can be identified on entry with reasonable accuracy. There is now enough, though very limited, experience with such programs to suggest that they offer the most direct and effective means for building immediately a small but significant impact of the university years on future leadership. Any new thrust, starting now in 1976, that will have the practical effect of producing more and better leaders by the year 2000, will have to take off fast—in the colleges and universities, but outside the normal faculty decision process. A strong trustee interest in seeing that this happens will give it a great assist.

3. The present arrangement that imposes the obligation for educating young people in institutions that are separated from "real life" and that permits the use and exploitation of the same people in another set of institutions for the production of goods and services should give way, regarding persons between 14 and 28, to a sharing of the opportunity and obligations between schools and employing institutions. Some at age 14 will develop better mostly in employment. Some, even up to age 28, will do better in schools. But none in that age range should be wholly in employment or in school. Several corollary conditions go with this assertion.

a. Since we are not likely to have 100 percent employment, those consigned to unemployment should be the oldest in the work force. From age 14 to 28, those who want to work should have that opportunity without exception. Both employers and unions will adapt to this. If anybody has to be unemployed, it should be the old rather than the young.

b. The obligation on employers is to provide developmental opportunities for the young. At age 28, given two persons with comparable potential to lead and manage, whether they have been in school or in work, their readiness for managerial responsibility should be approximately equal.

c. We know now that the mentors under whom young persons work can remarkably accelerate or seriously inhibit the growth of their understudies. And we know now how to prepare mentors for this important task. *All* young persons should have their initial work under a capable mentor—as a matter of right.

d. All of this will require a new work ethic in which it is accepted that, at least between the ages of 14 and 28, work exists as much for the growth fulfillment of individuals as it does for the production of goods and services or the reward of investors. And it will require of schools that they accept a new pedagogy in which gainful work is accepted on a par with academic experience as a developmental force.

4. My final response to the question *Who should do what to prepare managers for the year 2000?* is: We should get on with what we ought to be doing to prepare them for the year 1977. In addition to the above, let me state an urgent concern for the structure of our institutions—*all of them:* businesses, governments, churches, schools, hospitals, philanthropies. If anything is clear from my fifty years of institution-watching, it is this: By the anachronistic structure of our institutions that we so slavishly maintain, and by the incentives we place before people, we are killing off leaders and managers faster than we can possibly develop them. And if we do not stop this, the most heroic measures to prepare people for the unforeseeable conditions of the year 2000 will avail us little. Three brief suggestions for things to stop doing:

a. Trustees and directors of voluntary (nongovernmental) institutions will stop accepting the nominal and honorary roles designed for them by administrators and assert the *managing* role with which they are legally charged.

b. The hierarchical structure of administration with a single chief will be abandoned in favor of a collegial group that is *led* by a primus inter pares rather than *managed* by a chief executive officer. Trustees will design and staff the top administrative structure, not just let it evolve out of a competitive struggle.[1]

c. The ethic of competition will be muted in favor of the ethic of service as the prime motivator of institutional performance.

Trustees and directors, using the power they now have, can raise the quality of the total society faster than can any other means I know of. This is not said to denigrate the role of government. But

[1] For a fuller treatment of this concept, see R.K. Greenleaf, *The Institution as Servant* (Cambridge, Mass.: Center for Applied Studies, 1972).

in answer to the question *Who?*: Unequivocally, it is directors and trustees of voluntary institutions.

I have been assigned the question *Who should do what?*—not *how?* But I have enough confidence in the inventiveness, tenacity, and good will of most trustees and directors to believe that, *if enough of them really want to do these things, they will find a way.*

REDESIGN OF THE
EDUCATIONAL PROCESS

Greenleaf's proposal for carefully nurturing a select segment of the population during fourteen critical years is reminiscent of Plato's *Republic.* But Greenleaf's aim is to develop creative leaders for business enterprises and other independent institutions—not just "citizens" of the government.

Several aspects of the proposal are akin to points already made by Hubert. Both give strong emphasis to realism—a personal acquaintance with concrete facts of cooperative behavior; both suggest a mixture of experience and formal education; both are skeptical that university faculties and administrators will initiate the kind of redesign in the educational process that will be necessary to nurture innovative leadership.

For a still different view, let us turn to suggestions by W. Allen Wallis, Chancelor of the University of Rochester. Wallis, an eminent economic statistician, served as Dean of the University of Chicago's Graduate School of Business during a period of rapid growth. He maintains an active interest in business education while guiding a much wider range of activities in his present position.

by W. ALLEN WALLIS

EDUCATING FUTURE MANAGERS

To know what should be done now to prepare the managers, who will assume top responsibilities a quarter of a century hence, it is necessary to anticipate what the world will be like a quarter of a century hence.

Two things can be said about that. First, we certainly cannot tell now with either precision or certainty what the world will be like twenty-five years hence—much less forth years hence when the managers we educate today will be approaching retirement but still managing. Second, we can project with reasonable assurance a few broad trends likely to persist until 2000 and to be more important than now in the world the managers of 2000 will face. Each of these propositions leads to certain prescriptions for management education today.

A Broader Base

The first proposition, that we cannot be sure of much about 2000, means that we must emphasize *education* for management, not mere training. That is, we must emphasize not how-to-do-it nor even what-to-do, but broad principles and basic understanding. What-to-do and how-to-do-it can be learned as the years go by, as the environment for management evolves and as the specific circumstances of each individual manager's responsibilities take shape. These things can be learned much better if the manager's education has prepared him deliberately for lifelong learning from experience, than if it has trained him for the world he encounters and the job he takes upon leaving school.

Specifically, management education should be strong in economics, not just the economics of the firm but the economics of the economy, and even some of the history of the economy, including business history. Management education should be strong in political science and the actual working of politics, politicians, propaganda, and public opinion, and even some political history. It should be strong in behavioral sciences, including individual and social psychology, some psychiatry, and sociology. It should be strong in law and jurisprudence, including the actual working of lawyers, legislatures, and courts. It should be strong in quantitative methods, including mathematics, statistics, and computers. It should convey some comprehension of science and technology, including not only physical but also biological science.

These requirements are preposterous if viewed in the light of the standard two years available for an M.B.A. degree and of the fact that there must be room also for the distinctive core of management education: production, marketing, personnel, finance, and accounting. But the M.B.A. is preceded by a B.A., so the entire curriculum is really six years. The requirements enumerated above would be attainable if the entire six-year program were integrated, or at least coordinated.

So one change in management education that should be made immediately is to coordinate it better with undergraduate education, in order to come closer to covering the full range that should be encompassed in the preparation of managers for 2000. This might be done by specifying premanagement requirements, as medical schools specify premedical requirements. It might be done by a unified B.A.-M.B.A. program in which the last two undergraduate years and the two M.B.A. years become a single curriculum. No doubt there are many ways in which it could be done. In any event, far more time than two years is required, and the way to get the additional time is to make better use of the four undergraduate years—not, obviously, at the expense of liberal education, but as part of it.

Coping with Government Regulation

So much for the consequences of the fact we cannot tell now what the world will be like in 2000. What are the consequences of the second proposition—that a few broad trends seem likely to persist and so can be projected with at least a little confidence?

The most important and also the most certain of these trends, as the one with the greatest impact on managers, is the trend toward totalitarian government. This bicentennial year finds us scuttling at an ever-increasing pace what was accomplished two hundred years ago when mercantilism was scuttled. We are moving rapidly toward a neo-mercantilism in which the phrase "rule of law" is taking on a new and perverse meaning, that all relations between individuals should be regulated by law.

Managers increasingly will find themselves saddled by governments with costs that they have no way of recovering. Often it will be clear that the costs yield nothing of value, or at least nothing whose value to *anyone,* inside or outside the enterprise, is commensurate with their costs. Indeed, the costs usually will result from arbitrary edicts of middle- and low-level government employees; and these functionaries may have a preference for costly measures that have no appreciable consequences, for these create opportunities for mutually advantageous transactions between managers and officials in which no third parties are harmed.

Under the regime of government agencies such as the Environmental Protection Agency, the Occupational Safety and Health Administration, the Employees' Retirement Income Security Administration, and dozens of others, bribery and extortion will inevitably become even more pervasive than under local building codes and zoning regulations. Bribery and corruption will become as unavoidable as a part of management in this country as they are in Asia, South America, Eastern Europe, and most other parts of the world.

Many American managers have had to learn to live with this situation in other countries. How will they cope with it here? The very lives of the people will depend on managers' finding ways to continue to produce goods and services, distribute them, employ labor, and raise capital.

Probably one way of adapting to a regime dominated by corruption will be to turn activities over to the government. This will then leave the bribery and corruption directly between government officials and the public, without the intervention of managers.

Another trend that seems certain to persist until the year 2000 is the use of computers. Not only will things that are now done be done better and quicker, but things will be done that we cannot yet imagine. The manager of the future will not, of course, be his own computer expert, but he will require more than a superficial understanding of computer technology, especially "software" technology. Although leading schools of management now expose most students to computers, usually this exposure is simply to the computer as a tool in studying finance, accounting, and statistics. A worthwhile innovation now would be a course for all students dealing with computers and computer sciences.

VECTORS THAT
NEED DEVELOPMENT

For symposium panelists the proposals by Wallis and Greenleaf triggered many other suggestions. Greenleaf leaves much unspecified, and Wallis' apparent acceptance of bribery stirred sharp protests. On one point there was agreement—business schools can and should increase their efforts along several vectors in order to serve tomorrow's needs better. Complacency is unwarranted.

Fortunately, all schools need not do the same things. Just as product differentiation applies to aspiring managers, so too should institutions aiding managerial development provide distinctive kinds of help. Currently, the accreditation process has a tendency to push schools into the same mold; in the future we need more innovation and differentiation.

In the array of possible new directions, several will demand action. The need is so strong that someone will meet it. If at least some of the existing schools don't adapt to the emerging requirements, new institutions will step into the gap. This category of irrepressible future needs includes the following.

Continuing education

The pressure for providing education to people already in managerial positions will come from three trends. (a) Rapid change—explored in Part I—makes updating essential. A wide variety of fronts are involved: legal, social, economic, international, technological, political. (b) Relevance—that is, help in resolving current, demanding, real-life problems—becomes more important as expectations rise about the role managers should play (see pages 58–62). Continuing education can be a valuable aid to managers in meeting this challenge. (c) Efficiency is obtained by giving the education primarily (though perhaps not entirely) to those most likely to use it, and by a shorter time span between exposure and application.

Continuing education for managers involves much more than giving to persons in middle age existing courses intended for inexperienced students. Shorter modules designed for selected and experienced persons will be needed. Some of these modules can be closely tied to faculty research, provided that research is problem oriented. Teaching methods will have to be adjusted to differences in background and motivation of the more mature students. But all this special preparation will be warranted by the higher probability of significant use.

Professional certification

Additional forms of certification, beyond the M.B.A., will undoubtedly develop. The C.P.A. and C.L.U. are already well recognized, as are licensing tests for stockbrokers and engineers. The extension of equal-opportunity regulations into managerial ranks will encourage many more programs leading to certification of professional status. Business schools are natural agencies to provide the necessary academic training, if not the certification itself.

A tie of continuing education and professional certification is also developing. A number of states now require lawyers to take additional courses on recent changes in the law in order to maintain their professional status. A similar move is underway for nursing and other areas of health care. Public accounting is joining the movement; for example. California requires eighty hours of some sort of professional study every four years.

Legally required certification for managers would encounter many obstacles. However, voluntary certification in various fields related to managing is clearly in the offing.

Value standards

A different kind of thrust deals with values. Managers cannot escape tough value choices—choices in their personal behavior and choices among competing social goals. In the future even more than in the past, retention of a major managerial post will require wise value judgments.

Business schools, in turn, will not be permitted to continue their amoral posture. Pleading scientific objectivity is a cop-out. At a minimum, good schools should explore value issues frankly, then give students a framework for resolving hard choices. Moreover, those schools that elect to provide "professional" training must try to inculcate the ethics that are an integral part of that profession.

Diplomatic skill

Group confrontations will become increasingly common and troublesome, as we noted in Part I; and dealing with such confrontations calls for political (diplomatic) skill. Moreover, political insight will aid the enlarging number of managers who are actively involved with governmental regulation. And politics explain a significant part of what happens within a company and in industry associations. A manager lacking political skill has a serious handicap.

Politics are an unexplored dimension of managerial life. In the years ahead political skill will become more, not less, useful to managers. This is an area where some schools can pioneer with major impact and contribution.

Managing not-for-profit enterprises

A shift in the proportion of national resources—and managers—from agriculture and manufacturing to services is already recorded history. A parallel irrepressible rise in government operations—at local, state, and national levels—is occurring. Sharing in this growth of services and government are a host of not-for-profit enterprises.

These trends offer an unusual opportunity to at least some business schools. The processes of managing intangibles are similar but different from our customary models. Much of what we know can be transferred, but enough new must be added to make product differentiation desirable. Within universities new coalitions will emerge embracing business and other professional schools such as medicine, education, and social work. A few brave souls say that even a university itself is manageable.

We still have much to learn and teach about different management styles that are suited to particular settings.

The growth vectors just discussed—continuing education, professional certification, value standards, political skill, not-for-profit management—by no means exhaust the ways a business school may seek distinction. Hubert, Greenleaf, and Wallis sketch even sharper shifts in structure. The list does show that ample opportunity for innovation exists. And it is our basic thesis, based on the future predicted in Parts I, II, and III, that business education must innovate if it is to do its share in preparing managers for the year 2000-plus.

C. BUSINESS PRACTICES THAT WILL NURTURE MANAGERS FOR THE YEAR 2000

Many influences shape each individual manager. In adult life the most powerful influence typically is a manager's working environment—his immediate bosses, work assignments, team experiences, social support, rewards and punishments, and the like. Companies can deliberately design this working environment to some extent. Our interest here is what companies can do—within the design freedom they can muster—to help prepare managers to deal with the kinds of issues highlighted in Parts I, II, and III.

As a prelude to that discussion Harold Smiddy's contribution to the symposium is presented. This piece really stands by itself, because Smiddy points the finger at each of us individually. He is too wise to presume that either education or company actions can assure the self-imposed discipline that he believes is so vital. We include the essay in this section because it does stress quality of working relationships—and working relationships are an important aspect of most of the suggestions that will be presented later.

Smiddy has had a profound effect on management practice around the world. He was a primary architect of General Electric Company's management revolution of the 1950s, many features of which have been copied by all sorts of companies. He energetically participates in all the leading management associations, prodding esoteric model-builders and behavioral scientists alike. From this intimate understanding of such a wide array of management concepts, he selects voluntary teamwork as a quality urgently needed by tomorrow's managers.

by **HAROLD F. SMIDDY**

THE INDISPENSABILITY OF
VOLUNTARY TEAMWORK

The aim in asking for these comments is a "hope to identify major moves that should be initiated now in order to provide the kinds of managers society will need twenty-five years hence"—so that both business executives and educators can act accordingly.

Perhaps the *primary* need is for every individual to exercise self-discipline so that—as his work, interest, and information get more and more complex—he will give voluntary adequate current attention to his *teamwork* responsibilities as well as to his functional work, as such.

As knowledge grows greater in aggregate and more specialized for individuals, the requirement for more and more individuals to function in organized, increasingly complex, and steadily more inter-mixed institutions grows proportionately.

Present results prompt, more and more, the idea that voluntary teamwork responsibilities have to be sensed and heeded as such progress proceeds. The growing dangers if individuals fail to do so are widely appreciated. Perhaps just two quotations will make the point. In his little Doubleday Anchor book, *The Coming Dark Age: What Will Happen When Modern Technology Breaks Down?*, Roberto Vacca paints his picture pointedly:

My thesis is that our great technological systems of human organization and association are continuously outgrowing ordered control: they are now reaching critical dimensions of instability.

In the Annual Report of the American Arbitration Association, "The Growing Challenge," March 9, 1976, President Robert H. Coulson puts the present situation this way:

> The climate of the '70s has not been one of moderation. Individuals and institutions alike seem preoccupied with litigation, with confrontations, and with well-publicized refusals to move towards consensual arrangements. Intractable disagreements appear on every side: public employee strikes; class actions involving major enterprises; stalemates over the construction of needed public facilities; mass complaints swamping the government's remedial forums. A national appetite for hostility and violence may be a hopeless luxury at this point in time.

As the American Arbitration Association has fully sensed, classic facilities—including the whole court system—either to mediate, to arbitrate, or to legally settle disputes are more and more strained to their breaking points in more and more fields, topics, and nations; need for dispute *prevention* thus mounts.

Are the situation and the trend hopeless? No; human resources will sooner or later be able to control trends, reassert progress, and avoid or overcome collapse. This is what Arthur Koestler—after years of solid research—so hopefully found in his book of the late 1940s called *Insight and Outlook.*

But a couple of other long-known points have to be realized. Each individual must think and act responsibly, rather than just "worry" about it all; as the old quote goes, "Worry is a thin stream of fear, trickling through the mind, which unless checked will cut a deepening channel into which all other thoughts will be drained."

But logical and rational thought alone is not enough—even for individuals deeply familiar with "scientific management." The human mind has its rational side, but no less its moral, ethical, and even spiritual dimension too; and all need to be brought to bear by every individual, especially in many of today's less quantifiable confrontations and issues. The limits were nicely stated by Harry Arthur Hopf some years back, as he accepted the CIOS Gold Medal. Harry quoted what he called Malapert's dictum: "Science in the last analysis only makes us derive our ignorance from its ultimate depths."

So to conclude these highly personal views on "Who Should Do What to Prepare for the Year 2000?" it does seem that the primary need already falls on every one of us personally to exercise self-discipline in order to give adequate current attention to his teamwork responsibilities—no matter what his functional work or what institutions he participates in to carry it out. The alternative if each of us should not voluntarily do so would seem to be some terrible, overcentralized dictatorship, if only to keep such "law and order" as all of us deeply desire.

As the statesman Clemenceau of World War I put it: "Freedom is the right to discipline myself so I do not have to be disciplined by others."

COMPANY NOURISHMENT OF
FUTURE LEADERS

Two features of Smiddy's paper bear on our next concern. First, to emphasize his main point, Smiddy leaves to others a consideration of what *companies* should do to assist managers in acquiring attitudes and behavior patterns that they will sorely need. Second, he—like Bower and Greenleaf—presses for an immediate start. Voluntary teamwork, to continue that example, will be needed tomorrow as well as twenty-five years hence. So the time to start is now.

This stress on immediate need leaves a thorny question—will long-run managerial requirements indeed be met? The justification, of course, is that the particular proposal has continuing validity; it is good medicine now and it probably will be good in the uncertain future. Unfortunately, such short-run measures, while often also helpful in the longer run, may be inadequate. It is rather common for companies to find that senior managerial posts cannot be satisfactorily filled by promotion from within—an experience that suggests faulty resource development.[1]

On the other hand, we dare not think only of the long-run future. Unlike a forest that can be harvested a generation after planting, managers must be active throughout their careers. The art, of

[1] Occasionally death or other catastrophe upsets even well-planned managerial succession.

course, is to be preparing managers for the future with all the skill and foresight we can muster, while at the same time retaining these future managers in currently useful and challenging assignments.

Several proposals emerged from the symposium for company action directed toward the multiple purpose.

1. Monitor leadership development

The basic steps a company should take to assure itself a suitable reservoir of executive talent are well known. Bower has summarized these cogently (see pp. 51–54). He also observes that too often companies follow the form without facing the tough decisions necessary to make the system work well.

The procedure fits managers for the future. The specific qualifications sought and the aids to individual growth, however, must be adapted to include the new tasks we have been exploring. For instance, new ethics for business will require that revised standards be used in evaluating candidates. Rising expectations about managers' results will change the "pars" that are acceptable. The crux will be getting the new criteria understood and accepted in time.

2. Make change normal

Agility in responding to environmental changes is likely to be developed only in companies that treat change as a normal way of life. Just as we all expect the front page of a newspaper to change from day to day, company tradition may lead each manager to expect a substantial change in job content over any five-year period. This implies both an openness about one's role and skill in learning new ways.

Continuing education is an inherent factor in such a pattern of change. Managers and specialists must often retool, and companies can expedite the process by encourgaging—even insisting—that their key people use significant blocks of their time avoiding obsolescence. And for companies that want to pioneer, especially in high-technology areas, continuing education is imperative.

All forecasts point to frequent change in the future. But incessant change breeds inefficiency. We must allow the factory, the social organization, the individual to produce for a while before remodeling it. So as a practical matter there must be an adroit balance between agile change and periods of stability.

3. Reward "internal entrepreneurs"

As companies become larger and complex, and as government regulations shackle activities, innovation becomes increasingly difficult. In spite of company encouragement to change, an innovation requires someone to take the initiative. The bright idea needs a champion, a person willing to risk his reputation and some friendships, an individual who can inspire confidence and muster resources. This internal entrepreneur makes a unique, vital contribution and should be rewarded.

Encouraging internal entrepreneurs spurs executive development. In addition to the specific innovations launched, the process trains people in leadership; the skillful innovator is likely to become a prime candidate for a senior job.

4. Have managers participate in social planning

From society's viewpoint, business firms are resource converters (see page 61 for expansion of this concept), and each firm will be held accountable for how it treats employees, customers, the environment, investors, and other resource groups. Increasingly, a company will have to consider the plight of its resource contributors in terms only indirectly related to activities within its own facilities. This is its "social responsibility."

The wise company seeks to participate constructively in any planning that bears on its ability to meet the social responsibility thrust upon it. It can't duck out, so it should get in the act. Managers should be encouraged to participate in such social planning, either as representatives of the company or as private citizens. Through such participation they will learn more about social issues, and they will be better prepared to advise their companies on social action.

5. Provide training in diplomacy

Many of the social issues just referred to, much of the governmental regulation, and some of the actions within a company itself are greatly influenced by political processes. Group confrontations are strongly political in nature. However, our Western culture and training emphasize rational decision making. Rational analysis is indeed vital, but often it is inadequate. To understand how many decisions get made, and to influence the outcomes, managers need diplomatic (*political*) skill.

Since most managers are schooled in rational analysis but have given little serious thought to diplomacy, companies should provide assistance in learning the art of a diplomat.

6. Make explicit use of different management styles

No one management style is best for all situations. Running a subway system calls for quite different planning, organization, controls, and motivation than does a research laboratory. In the future, as the pressures on managers increase and expectations of results become more demanding, the selection of a management style suited to the particular activity being managed will become more crucial. Fine-tuning must replace fads.

Among the questions involved in selecting management styles is when computers are vital and when a burden. Matrix organization solves some managerial dilemmas but in other circumstances creates havoc. Job enrichment appeals to some workers, while others become confused and frustrated. Service industries pose measurement and reward problems not present in clothing manufacture. These examples suggest the sophistication needed to manage wisely. Variations are necessary within companies as well as between industries.

If managers are taught not just "how we do it here" but also when to use variations, they will be much better prepared to deal with the changes that lie ahead. They will then be able to adjust the design to fit new situations.

None of the suggestions above is brand new; most companies have started on the way. Nevertheless, any firm seriously concerned about what it might do to prepare managers for the year 2000 (and before) will find these propositions provocative: monitor leadership development—especially in terms of future needs, make change a normal way of life, reward "internal entrepreneurs," have managers participate in social planning, provide training in diplomacy, and make explicit use of different management styles. Managers who receive this kind of nourishment will be good bets for future leaders.

CONCLUSION

IRREPRESSIBLE OPPORTUNITIES

Several issues keep recurring in the preceding analyses. They provide a useful focus to summarize many, though not all, of the suggestions made throughout this book about preparing managers for the years ahead. These issues reflect a set of pressures that will surely plague enterprise managers from now until 2000; we can't escape them. But we can view them as opportunities, because those companies and universities that respond constructively will have turned potential trouble into an asset.

Progressive Reorientation

Doubts are being raised about future "growth," but no one questions the prevalence of change. Possibly we will have to slow down our total consumption of energy, for example, but we still must adjust to massive shifts in our sources of energy. Similar churning beneath the surface will occur within a gradually stabilizing population, where we may experience a boom in retirees and empty classrooms. Military budgets are likely to rise and fall in much larger swings than the GNP.

The forecasts in the body of this report, in fact, anticipate substantial overall growth. More pertinent to managers of enterprises is the prospect of a lot of stress and strain within the process of moving

119

ahead. For instance, Gordon predicts rapid advances in the application of microelectronics and in the medical field, but serious obstacles in getting food and raw materials from available sources to
points of need.

Two aspects of this future change deserve emphasis. First is its
pervasiveness. New technology is only one source of disruption. Political institutions, lifestyles, sources of power, religion, willingness to
work, inflation, and military might are also being transformed. The
future manager will have to be as alert to shifts in personal values as
to cuts in competitors' costs. The whole social fabric is being re-
woven.

Second, even where we feel confident that a predicted change
will occur, its ramifications are hard to foresee. For instance, if public concern about safety stymies atomic energy development, U.S.
dependence on foreign oil will rise; what then will OPEC nations do?
Will U.S. support of Israel decline? Will balance-of-payment problems undercut our ability to obtain ore or orchids from developing
countries? As another example, New York City's effort to assume a
sound financial posture affects not only its employees and suppliers; municipal credit of other cities can be bolstered or under-
mined, directly affecting their ability to deal with urban blight and
indirectly affecting local unemployment. Thus, in our interacting
system, a strain or opportunity at one spot sparks responses, and
these responses breed further responses. We know that ripple effects
will occur but can't be sure just what form they will take.

What can be done to prepare managers to deal with these frequent, pervasive changes? Wallis proposes an integrated six-year
undergraduate-M.B.A. program that gives students a strong grounding
in economics, political science, behavioral science, law, and quantitative methods; this base is to prepare future managers for lifelong
learning from experience.

Another tack is continuing education—probably part-time
courses or intensive short-term programs spaced intermittently over
a manager's entire career. This education could deal with any aspect
of the environment that is changing in significant respects; it should
include both specific how-to measures for grappling with new phenomena, and basic frameworks that help managers analyze and predict what is likely to happen in new circumstances.

Providing education on a continuing though intermittent basis offers several advantages. (1) Updating on recent developments in key areas can be provided in depth. (2) Closer relevance of the material to the then-current managerial problems enhances interest and understanding. (3) Efficiency of training is increased sharply by giving the courses (primarily) to those most likely to use them and by shortening the time span between exposure and application.

The aim is to progressively reorient managers to the changing world in which they work. Much more than factual information is involved. New frames of reference, self-assurance, and revised skills will often be needed.

A continuing education program actively supported by companies will establish an attitude—a widespread presumption—that intellectual retooling is normal. In high-technology fields, seminars and other continuing training devices are already common. This practice should be expanded; the attitude should be: "Of course managers go back to school"—not primarily for promotion but to stay abreast of the times.

Such periodic exposures to fresh material can have a favorable effect on morale. A kind of "job enrichment" is provided. The presumption is that most managers' jobs will keep changing and that managers will share the stimulation of learning and playing in a new ballgame.

Moreover, common use of continuing education will ease the task of dealing with "plateaued managers"—those who have resigned themselves to getting by in their present jobs. Changing to new careers will become more common (and necessary), and the mechanisms for preparing such shifts—within or outside the company—will be readily available.

Whether universities will be flexible enough in their staffing, product packaging, and teaching methods to serve this continuing education market is far from clear. If they don't, other organizations will—e.g., trade associations, consultants, profit-making schools.

Managers as Diplomats

One change already evident and on the increase is more reliance on politics. The political process—in contrast to rational analysis—is being used more and more by both companies and governments to arrive at important decisions.

Group confrontations contribute to this trend. Not only labor unions but pressure groups of all sorts—Women's Lib, consumer groups, community associations, Sierra Club, ecology buffs, NAACP, and many others—are pushing for their particular aims. Tactics include demonstrations, sit-ins, boycotts, picketing, and other blocking of action. These groups are primarily political organizations that rally around a cause, and they must be dealt with in a political rather than a rational, analytical fashion.

The political process is also found in other kinds of situations. Clearly, receiving approval for variable annuities involved the major insurance companies, investment bankers, and regulatory agencies in a whole series of maneuvers and coalitions. A similar process surrounds the offering of checking accounts by savings banks—and the extension of branch banking.

Any company that tries to build a new storage facility for liquefied gas will encounter a series of hurdles quite aside from the economics of the proposed location; local groups concerned about ecology, safety, employment, parks, and home heating will enter the fray. And shutting down a plant stirs up another set of legitimate, self-interest actions—especially if the plant is a relatively large employer or an outpost of a multinational company in a developing country. Political skill is essential to action in all such situations.

The movement is toward even more political activity. Increasing interdependence, reliance on governmental aid and regulation, insistence that all views be heard, legal endorsement of unions and other bargaining groups, public recognition of the power of group pressure—all tend to politicize cooperative activity.

In the political process each key person pushes for his particular cause, yet he recognizes that he must gain the support of other key persons who have their own goals. Favors, power, coalitions, delaying actions, face-savings, depolarization, restating issues, concessions are all part of the game. Typically the players expect to have continuing relationships with each other, and this tempers their moves.

Politics within companies are not unknown. Although the preceding examples arise in external dealings, powerful individuals inside an organization may be committed to a cause (possibly their own careers) and resort to politics to achieve it. For example, in one breakfast food company a decision to also sell dog food involved a

long political fight. Similarly, a prominent university dropped inter-
collegiate football only after a whole series of internal political
maneuvers.

Most managers regard politics as being a bit sordid. As with sex
a generation ago, a person might indulge in it often but it was not a
topic for polite conversation. This attitude toward politics arises
from our reverence for the scientific method and rational analysis.
We just hate to admit that any of our decisions were made by any
method other than rational, logical choice.

Now, if politics are going to become more and more common—as contended above—managers should become skilled in the
process. Instead of acting aloof, they should study its elements, observe what works when, recognize when it is the best way to secure
cooperation, and turn an inevitable practice to constructive purposes.

Managers will be better equipped to deal with tough problems
ahead if educational institutions give significant attention to the political process and if companies include politics as one of the skills
they expect managers to possess. As a gesture toward building respec-
tability for this ancient art, the heading of this section refers to managers as "diplomats"—not mere politicians!

Advancement and Protection via Certification

The pressures on managers are rising and, as we have noted,
these further demands will result in some shifting in managerial qualifications most prized. Response to these pressures will be complicated by an oversupply of people seeking managerial jobs. The oversupply is likely to be vocal and troublesome.

Candidates for managerial jobs are cropping up faster than the
openings. Women and members of minorities are moving into positions formerly held only by white males. The numbers of people
studying business administration in college is on the upswing, and at
the graduate level there has been a fourfold increase in M.B.A.s during the last decade; by the late 70's, 11 percent of all master's degrees were M.B.A.s.

Aspirations are high. The training these people receive is focused on management. Company recruiters talk of promotion opportunities. Most students who select and make sacrifices to study the
business field consider it a stepping stone into managerial positions.

These thousands of new candidates may not, in fact, have all the qualifications that will be needed in the future, but their hopes and expectations center on upper middle management and senior management positions.

There will be some more managerial jobs in the future. As we automate services and production, the proportion of total employees considered to be "managers" (staff as well as line) will rise somewhat. However, openings will increase at a much slower rate than the surge of aspiring candidates. The competition for good managerial jobs will become very tough indeed.

In the resulting scrambling for positions legal rights will become more of an issue. "Fair employment practices" will be pushed up the hierarchy of jobs. When filling a position companies will have to be able to show that they did not discriminate on a basis of sex, race, religion—and perhaps age, residence, marital status, school tie, political party, country of birth, size, family, and other distinctions that have not yet surfaced.

The aim of such legal constraints is fairness in selection. Some candidates who are having difficulty fulfilling their aspirations will insist on their rights. And this will add complexity, delay, and rigidity to the whole executive development process.

A second result of oversupply will be more attention to professional certification. By being certified a person seeks to differentiate himself from competitors. Historically, professional certifications arose to project consumers who are unable to judge the quality of the services they receive—for example, in medicine, law, engineering, accounting, plumbing, electrical work, and the like. However, a diploma, degree, or license can also serve as a selection device.

Certification will probably be used increasingly to identify, and reduce, the eligible contenders for a position. The possibilities here run in many directions. A person may be certified in a subject such as Japan or laser beams. Or the specialty may be an aspect of managing such as O.D. (organization development), M.I.S. (management information systems), PERT/Cost, corporate planning, control in transnational companies, or executive compensation. Note that a high degree of proficiency in the fields just cited is more likely to be a desired qualification in filling a staff job than a line job. Nevertheless, in conditions of oversupply any relevant basis to distinguish (discriminate) among candidates may be highlighted.

Updating is a further development in certification. A specialist well trained today may be obsolete ten or fifteen years later—as we noted in Part I. In an effort to ensure that members keep abreast of changing environment and new insights, a few professions are requiring additional training every few years to maintain certification. For example, lawyers in some states must pass courses dealing with recent legislation. C.P.A.s in California have to spend a minimum number of hours every four years in training to retain their professional status. Here we find "progressive reorientation," discussed above, tied into professional certification.

Although certification is unlikely to be *required* for all managers during this century, voluntary moves in this direction will surely increase. Just as teachers often receive salary increments when they take additional training, companies may encourage formal updating. Individuals will seek certificates of various kinds, partly for their own self-respect and more specifically as a way of favorably differentiating the services they offer.

Moral Managers

Between now and the year 2000 managers will find themselves increasingly involved in value issues. Two levels of conduct are in transition—personal ethics and the values used in company decisions.

Scandals reported in the newspaper headlines often entail a known violation of law or integrity. Possibly managers will become even more cynical about the need to observe established codes, but the tide appears to be running the other way. To retain a position in a public company, ethical behavior is becoming a *sine qua non*—if for no other reason than the serious consequences of doing otherwise.

Where the line between ethical and unethical lies, however, is often not clear. When does courtesy become bribery? How aloof must one keep to avoid conflict of interest? Is loyalty to family and friends ever warranted? In transnational work whose customs should be observed? The answer to such questions as these have changed during the past quarter-century, and they will continue to evolve during the next. And, difficult though it may be, we are going to expect future managers to be sensitive to these changes and adjust their personal behavior accordingly.

The values managers use in making decisions for their companies pose even more complications. Three forces plague the manager. (1) Society's expectations for results that managers produce are high and rising. For instance, quality products, intriguing jobs, no pollution, steady employment for more workers, and stable prices are now added to rising profits as important goals. If managers hope to retain freedom to act, they cannot disregard these rising expectations. (2) Past actions are being judged by today's standards. Opening the West now brings condemnation from conservationists; protecting women workers is now illegal discrimination; state-approved disposition of waste is now subject to fine for pollution. This kind of reformer's morality is likely to continue to prevail. (3) The convenient single overriding goal of "profit maximization" is no longer generally acceptable to the public—and public endorsement is essential for any institution as vital and powerful as business enterprises.

This array of externally imposed standards puts managers on the spot. Managers cannot meet all expectations, and the guide for resolving conflicting demands that they used in the past—profits—is no longer considered adequate. Some more adaptable guide for setting values is needed.

The "resource converter" model offers an approach for setting values in the future. As explained on page 61, this model proposes that the basic function of managers in society is to convert resources (manpower, materials, capital, know-how, community infrastructure, capacity to consume) into outputs (goods, services, wages, taxes, etc.). Each resource contributor is induced to cooperate—typically on a continuing basis—by sharing in the output. The managers are the middlemen who keep the conversion process going. They negotiate deals with each resource contributor that are fitted as nearly as is practical to that contributor's desires and yet are viable for the enterprise as a whole. For the investor this deal involves some acceptable combination of interest, profit, liquidity, risk, capital gain, and the like; for labor the deal involves wages, attractive work, fringe benefits, security, etc.; for the community the deal involves taxes, local employment, minimum pollution, support of schools, and so forth; and likewise for each contributor.

As a resource converter the manager is cast in a role that is clearly vital to society. He is not a protagonist for any one resource group. Instead, the social values that the manager seeks to satisfy when he makes decisions for his company are the values of all the various resource contributors.

Of course, two crucial and complicating factors qualify this simplified source of values. First, all wishes of contributors cannot possibly be met. So the manager finds himself in the center of controversy over what is feasible. For instance, when an electric utility manager balances consumers' desire for instant power with ecologists' desire for undisturbed rivers with Treasury officials' desire to cut oil imports to save foreign exchange—he is immersed in social-value questions. Basically, however, he serves as a mediator, because his primary concern is keeping his utility running. The successful mediator is sensitive to the relative weight of desires of each party and can fashion a realistic, acceptable proposal.

Second, the desires of resource contributors change. An acceptable package this year is unsatisfactory next year—"progress" is an ingrained concept. This means that an alert manager who wishes to keep his enterprise operating without serious disruption must anticipate new requests and try to devise ways of meeting them or channelling them into feasible alternatives. Thus, the manager is an active participant in shifting values.

In this framework the manager is no reluctant Scrooge. Rather, his success depends to a large extent on how well he perceives value issues and how ingenious he is in meeting highest priorities. He is moral because he is responsive to human wants.

Picturing the manager as a resource converter at least emphasizes one point—future managers will be inextricably concerned with change in social values. Even the reader who draws back from this particular model must recognize how immersed managers are in the process of altering social values. Both schools and companies should prepare future managers for this important and delicate part of their jobs.

Internal Entrepreneurs

Future managers will need to attend to many matters. In addition to the array of problems with which they currently wrestle, they will have to devote more time to the topics sketched in the preceding pages. Progressive reorientation, diplomacy, pressure from professionals, and changing values all will require energy and reflective thought. Life for a manager promises to be stimulating, demanding, and very busy indeed.

To this picture we must add growing government regulation.

Worldwide there is a trend to turn to governments to prevent, to guide, to stimulate—in almost every feature of life. As our activities become more interdependent, suggestions for regulation come from more sources. As we speed up our capacity to turn out reports, we ask for more. As we expand and refine our concept of a good life, we extend the arm of government. And the end is not in sight.

Such regulation tends to stifle innovation. Each proposed advance will in the future run up against more formal regulations that must be modified. Soon hiring a person for a newly designed job, for example, will be as difficult as securing a modification in a local building code. Even for experiments, more approvals will be demanded and more protections required. Also remember that the further removed a regulator is from the place where a change is contemplated, the more intransigent he becomes.

Internal entrepreneurs will be required to buck this trend. These are individuals who champion a bright idea. They take initiative long before a particular change is forced upon the company by outside developments. In promoting the idea they risk their personal reputation on its success, and they annoy people who are happy with the status quo. They must inspire enough confidence in their proposition to muster resources. They are true entrepreneurs, but they operate within the tangled web of a regulated organization.

Even enterprises that keep their staff oriented to a shifting environment will need internal entrepreneurs. They spark change. They are the leaven that turns available ingredients into new, constructive services.

Not all managers have to be entrepreneurs. But if our many enterprises are to be innovative in the kind of world that lies ahead, we must adjust our organizations and incentives so that a good sprinkling of internal entrepreneurs can flourish.

Opportunities for Distinction (Summary)

Our present managers are among the best in the world. Nothing in the preceding analysis of managers for 2000 indicates a complete reversal or scrapping of our present development processes. Personal qualifications now prized and cultivated will continue to be useful. Instead, the signs point sharply to refinement, more effort, and new emphasis.

Vital among the changes that should be made in our present practice are:

1. More emphasis and new ways of *reorientation,* so that managers on the job can keep abreast of a fast-changing environment. Continuing education, rather than prolonged schooling, has great advantages for this purpose.

2. Objective, constructive training in *diplomacy* (politics). This involves recognition of another dimension of managing along with rational analysis and behavioral science.

3. A wider range and improved quality of *professional certification.* More opportunities should be provided for new certifications in mid-career as well as for updating certifications received a decade or more earlier.

4. Direct confrontation of *value issues* and development of professional norms for action. Academic aloofness will no longer be tenable; the profit-maximization maxim has to be broadened if our pluralistic economy is to survive.

5. More deliberate encouragement of *internal entrepreneurs.* To counteract inevitable regulation and growing rigidities, more explicit support of internal innovators will be necessary.

Some companies and some educational institutions will take the lead in these new directions, and they will win distinction by doing so.

A wise counselor was asked, "If you had to use a single guide for selecting managers, what would it be?" He replied, "Tell me what the person does when he wakes up shivering in the middle of the night. If he merely pulls the covers he has over his head and hopes the cold will go away, I don't want him. If he climbs out of bed into the cold room and gets another blanket, he has potential." As educators and executives we face a similar choice when thinking about managers for the year 2000. We can rely on present practice and hope to get by, or we can treat the pressures ahead as a challenge and devise ways to harness them.

Selected References

A. NEW PRESSURES ON MANAGERS

Cassell, F.H., "The Politics of Public-Private Management," *MSU Business Topics,* Summer 1972. The shifting balance in government–business relations and a new social contract are confronting managers with an array of conflicting priorities.

Chapman, R.L., and F.N. Cleveland, "The Changing Character of the Public Service and the Administrator of the 1980s," *Public Administration Review,* July 1973. Anticipated pressures and changes affecting public managers, based on extensive study conducted for the National Academy of Public Administration; many of the anticipated changes also affect private managers.

Greenleaf, R.K., *The Servant as Leader.* (Cambridge, Mass.: Center for Applied Studies, 1973). Insightful essay on the interaction between leadership and service, especially helpful for future managers of our large enterprises.

Moffitt, D., ed., *America Tomorrow.* (New York: AMACOM, 1977). A series of articles looking forward to the year 2000, written by leading futurists for *The Wall Street Journal.* Topics include values, lifestyles, health, food, energy, housing, and transportation.

Paluszek, V.L., *Business and Society: 1976–2000.* (New York: AMACOM, 1976). Report on corporate social responsibility, based on the views of over 600 company presidents concerning the emerging business environment.

White House Conference, *A Look at Business in 1990.* (Washington: U.S. Government Printing Office, 1972). Papers and commentary on "the industrial world ahead"; chapters deal with technology and resources, the human side of enterprise, structure of the private enterprise system, world business, and social responsibility.

B. NEW SOURCES OF MANAGEMENT TALENT

Bach, G.L., "Whither Education for Business: 1950–2000?" *AACSB Bulletin,* Annual Report, 1975. The Dean of a pioneering business school during the third quarter of the present century outlines challenges for business education during the next twenty-five years.

Burck, C.G., "A Group Profile of the Fortune 500 Chief Executives," *Fortune,* May 1976. Comparison of the origins, education, experience, and interests of today's chief executives with those who headed our leading companies in 1955.

The Conference Board, *Education in Industry.* (New York: 1977). An intensive study of in-house education for company employees in 1977, when over 4,000,000 employees were taking company-run courses.

Patton, A., "The Coming Flood of Young Executives," *Harvard Business Review,* September 1976. The shift in post-war birth rates will result in a 45 percent increase in young potential executives by 1985, with accompanying problems of selection, motivation, and perhaps union organization in the lower managerial ranks.

Revans, R.W., *Developing Effective Managers, a New Approach to Business Education.* (New York: Praeger Publishers, 1971). Presents the theory and experience with "action-learning" by one of the leading European management education centers— Fondation Industrie–Université of Belgium; the focus is on continuing education for experienced managers.

Schon, D.A., "Deutero-Learning in Organizations: Learning for Increased Effectiveness," *Organization Dynamics,* Summer 1975.
Organizations, like individual managers, must learn how they
can best adjust to rapid change. This process, Schon contends,
calls for double-loop learning from experience as organizations
confront unprecedented problems.